Esther Present Truth Church

"For Such A Time Like This"

Books By Michael Scantlebury

The Fortress Church
Called to Be An Apostle – An Autobiography
Leaven Revealed
"I Will Build My Church." – Jesus Christ
Five Pillars of The Apostolic
Apostolic Purity
Apostolic Reformation
Internal Reformation
Jesus Christ The Apostle and High Priest of Our Profession
Kingdom Advancing Prayer – Volume I
Kingdom Advancing Prayer – Volume II
Kingdom Advancing Prayer – Volume III
God's Nature Expressed Through His Names
Identifying and Defeating The Jezebel Spirit

Available from Word Alive Press: wordalivepress.ca

ESTHER: PRESENT TRUTH CHURCH

Michael Scantlebury has taken author's prerogative in capitalizing certain words that are not usually capitalized according to standard grammatical practice. Also, please note that the name satan and related names are not capitalized as we choose not to acknowledge him, even to the point of disregarding standard grammatical practice.

Editorial Consultant: Anita Thompson – (604) 521-6042

Cover design by: Michelle Soon – (604) 789-9746

ISBN: 978-1-4866-0118-9

Word Alive Press
131 Cordite Road, Winnipeg, MB R3W 1S1
www.wordalivepress.ca

WORD ALIVE PRESS
Just Write!

Cataloging in Publication information may be obtained through Library and Archives Canada

Table Of Contents

Dedication

I would like to first of all dedicate this book to the Apostle and High Priest of my confession, Jesus Christ. I am truly grateful to Him for granting me the Grace to write this book. More specifically it is dedicated to my wife Sandra for her tireless support and commitment to God's purpose and to our children Candice, Rachel and Samuel who have been standing with me in the ministry. They understood as I spent countless hours writing this book.

Also to the family of Believers at Dominion-Life International Ministries, who gave me the opportunity to minister much of what is in this book as it became clear to me. To all the Leaders in the Body of Christ who have fought to gain and maintain Present Truth. Also to those in the Body of Christ who decided that they would follow their leaders as they made the journey into Present Truth and had the courage to stand with them as they did.

FOREWORD

In a season where the Church co-exists harmoniously with truth and error, this book provides us with a precision tool and well-calibrated instrument of change that is able to fine-tune the global Body of Christ.

The Body of Christ needs to shift into the present season of truth from its former antiquated, inaccurate religious position. The reality of truth is that it is not merely a concept but a person who is the absolute embodiment of our Lord Jesus Christ. In this book, Apostle Michael Scantlebury is a wise master builder who carries a heavenly technology and perspective on how we as the global Body of Christ need to function and migrate towards this Person of truth. He carries a burden to see truth manifest in the Body of Christ and also reveals the irregularities and spiritual parallels inside. He uses Esther as a platform and starting point to unpack the various spiritual deficiencies in the Body of Christ. Like Esther our passion must not give power to fear or control, we must see the Church in its natural glorious state. There is a poignant cry for corporate and personal purity and to keep the leaven out that will cause us to lose the glory of our lord Jesus Christ as Scantlebury so effortlessly articulates below:

"So it is as long as we keep pressing on in the things of God and keep ourselves from the corrupting influences of the world, the flesh and the devil, we will be free of leaven (sin and corruption)."

God's method of operating is through seasons, in the epoch of Samuel you cannot call upon Moses. We have come to the realization that there are many church leaders who are in one season whilst still living out another season. There must be a company of people that can tap into the mind of the Lord and translate with a bold declaration what season he is pronouncing upon His Body. This is the time of the Apostolic-Prophetic mandate that we are functioning in. Apostle Scantlebury like a skilled spiritual surgeon dissects the feasts with a steady hand and throws light upon every facet with such competence and delicate dexterity. He unveils our true nature as the Church and cements our position on the earth as an apostolic people.

Scantlebury emphases the life and practices of Esther and brings such clarity to her life as he mirrors it upon the present day church that we are able to clearly see what our reflection ought to look like. He takes us back to foundational doctrine discussing who Christ is and cites so effortlessly the ethical platforms and distinguishable characteristics that must be formed inside of our Apostles and their ministries.

Many are perplexed regarding what a Present Truth Church should look like and how a Present Truth Church must function. Present truth is also a term that we use to communicate the present process of revelation that currently defines the course of our spiritual experience. The purpose of present truth or current revelation from God is not that we build denominations or moves around them but that we become transformed according to that revelation. This means that we should seek out to find out what exactly God is speaking to us and to possess the ability to shift our paradigms of thought when he speaks a "new thing".

It is imperative that the global Church of Christ under-stands and embraces the Feast of Tabernacles in this apostolic and prophetic season. This feast is connected with the children of Israel having to leave their own homes and gathering together as a one unified man in tents. This is not a gathering for the sake of just coming together to show solidarity but rather a deep inward spiritual relocation of our salvation to the true head of the Church, Christ. It is in this place that we are instructed and taught His ways, which becomes the everlasting delight of our existence through the power of the Holy Spirit. It is a place of overflowing joy when we become a people who are fully dependent on his provision and sustenance.

During this Feast people danced whilst sounding the trumpet to give thanks to God for their yearly harvest. These acts being prophetic in nature is seen as the ultimate call to impact and invade the nations of earth ushering the fulfilment of the apostolic great commission to go into the nations make disciples through the unadulterated preaching of the good news.

Eschatology is often misunderstood therefore much clarity is needed in the Church. We will build and behave according to our understanding of the end times hence this must be set in order with urgency or we will lose focus of the pressing needs upon the Lord's heart and perambulate around the peripheral issues in the Kingdom. The right eschatological framework is crucial and paramount in this season of hype and sensationalism. There is an absolute need for proper interpretation of Scripture with a sober approach free of toxic teachings that pervade among the global Body of Christ.

To detoxify the Body Scantlebury zooms in on Matthew Chapter 24 and superimposes on truth shaping his lens to focus on truth removing our distorted vision in order to correctly see the blueprint in this Chapter. This is done in a systematic fashion that overthrows all false doctrines and builds the picture of what Christ was after He spoke the words found in this Chapter. There are profound truths that he peels layer upon layer until you are able to see the truth and can no longer contest his argument. Hats off for the time and effort he took to make darkness clear with light!

Apostle Michael Scantlebury reminds us that we are sons of God and not just mere sons of God but sons of the New Covenant. He takes the time to highlight the identity of a son and slave. He helps us see that we are priests and kings who must walk according to the desires of the Spirit and not the flesh and that submission and yielding together with the Holy Spirit is our birthright.

I highly recommend the author and this book to leaders and Saints globally who want to know the truth! He is a master marksman who has seen the enemy of truth and tracked him with the illumination of the Spirit. He takes his time looking down his scope to stalk stealthily every movement of false positions, teachings and doctrines and pulls the trigger with overwhelming confidence resulting in a kill shot. This is a hard hitting, spirit stirring and eye opening treasure trove of truth.

Apostle Robert Munien
Founder of Grace Outreach Ministries
grace-outreach.net
Durban, South Africa

Chapter One

A Time for Change

The Book of Esther is rich with revelation that is still valid and applicable for the day in which we live. Hidden within its pages is a powerful "present truth" message in it (which will be expounded on in chapter five). The lives of the people involved and the conditions that are seen have spiritual parallels for the Church. Our destiny as the Body of Christ is revealed. The preparations and conditions we must attain to are all similar.

From the onset of this book I wish to set out some of the typology that will be used. Jesus Christ is seen in the Book of Esther as the King. Please note that although in reality Ahasuerus was a carnal king in the book of Esther, in typology Ahasuerus represents the Lord Jesus Christ. Another example of this typology is the reference made of King Cyrus who was a heathen king but was still called God's anointed—Isaiah 45:1-5.

> "Thus says the LORD to His anointed, To Cyrus, whose right hand I have held--To subdue nations before him And loose the armour of kings, To open before him the double doors, So that the gates will not be shut: 2 'I will go before you And make

> the crooked places straight; I will break in pieces the gates of bronze And cut the bars of iron. 3 I will give you the treasures of darkness And hidden riches of secret places, That you may know that I, the LORD, Who call you by your name, Am the God of Israel. 4 For Jacob My servant's sake, And Israel My elect, I have even called you by your name; I have named you, though you have not known Me. 5 I am the LORD, and there is no other; There is no God besides Me. I will gird you, though you have not known Me."

It is also important to note the meaning of the name of king Ahasuerus. The Hebrew word for his name is "Achashwerosh and it means—lion, the king, mighty eye or mighty man." We can also see Queen Vashti, whose name is translated—one who is desired, beautiful woman, fair, lovely and belle. In typology she is seen as that of the "Old Order", that which is passing away to give place to the new or "present-truth". This can be seen or represented by the following chart, which we will get into the depth of in chapter seven of this book, dealing with the dimensions of the bondwoman and the freewoman described in Galatians Chapter 4.

OLD ORDER—LAW	NEW ORDER—GRACE
Bondwoman of Galatians 4	Freewoman of Galatians 4
Cain	Abel
Hagar	Sarah
Leah	Rachel
Peninnah	Hannah
Naomi	Ruth
Vashti (Israel)	Esther (Church)
Earthly Jerusalem	Heavenly Jerusalem
Old Covenant	New Covenant
Bondage	Freedom/Liberty
Law of sin and death	Law of the Spirit of Life
Harlot of Revelation 17-18	Bride of Revelation 19

As with every good story whether fictional or true, there must a villain, a hero, potential victims and a damsel! This true account of the lives of the Jewish people is no different and holds tremendous intrigue, drama and suspense and has some powerful truths for the New Testament Church.

Israel had been living in captivity, having been taken to Babylon by Nebuchadnezzar. They had been idolatrous and paid a heavy price for it with seventy years of captivity within the depraved Babylonian system. Ahasuerus was king when Esther was taken into his harem. It is generally believed that this Ahasuerus was in fact King Xerxes the first, the king of Persia who succeeded Darius I in 485 BC. His wife Queen Vashti was beautiful to look at, but likewise she was also very rebellious. Her defiance cost her the throne rights, and as a result the king wanted a suitable replacement. The person to replace her had to be beautiful and a virgin—Esther 2:2. Likewise, the Church must be the same—beautiful and pure.

Three main characters emerge in this story: Mordecai, Haman, and Esther. Their struggle and its outcome shadow a present day truth of the Church's conflict and destiny. Like Esther, our goal is to be in the presence of the King, in the throne room, with His sceptre extended in favour towards us.

Let's Start With The Villain—Haman

Haman was an evil oppressor and was the chief minister to the king. Just as satan thwarts the purposes of God in the life of the Believer where he seeks to destroy the Christian, Haman likewise wished for the destruction of all of God's people. As we research Haman we realize that he was of Amalekite descent. The Amalekites are the people who destroyed the Israelites as they journeyed from Egypt to the Promised Land and the Lord swore that He would eternally war against them! For purposes of clarity, I would like for us to briefly re-visit that account on Amalek—Exodus 17:8-16.

> "Now Amalek came and fought with Israel in Rephidim. 9 And Moses said to Joshua, "Choose us some men and go out, fight with Amalek. Tomorrow I will stand on the top of the hill

with the rod of God in my hand." 10 So Joshua did as Moses said to him, and fought with Amalek. And Moses, Aaron, and Hur went up to the top of the hill. 11 And so it was, when Moses held up his hand, that Israel prevailed; and when he let down his hand, Amalek prevailed. 12 But Moses' hands became heavy; so they took a stone and put it under him, and he sat on it. And Aaron and Hur supported his hands, one on one side, and the other on the other side; and his hands were steady until the going down of the sun. 13 So Joshua defeated Amalek and his people with the edge of the sword. 14 Then the LORD said to Moses, "Write this for a memorial in the book and recount it in the hearing of Joshua, that I will utterly blot out the remembrance of Amalek from under heaven." 15 And Moses built an altar and called its name, The-Lord-Is-My-Banner; 16 for he said, "Because the LORD has sworn: the LORD will have war with Amalek from generation to generation."

Some observations about Amalek/Amalekites

1. The Amalakites were descendants of Amalek—Son of Eliphaz who was Esau's firstborn son. In essence Amalek was Esau's grandson.
2. Remember that Esau was Jacob's firstborn son who sold his birthright for a morsel of meat (flesh); so it is no wonder that the Amalakites came through his lineage.
3. The Amalekites represent the "Flesh".
4. They were old enemies of Israel—They were allies of the Midianites who were responsible for the destruction of the produce of the Israelites, and were directly responsible for reducing them to poverty as recorded in Judges 6:3-4.
5. They represent a satanic strategy of destroying those who do not walk strongly and securely in the purposes of God as recorded in Deuteronomy 25:17–18.
6. They were a menace and a thorn in the flesh of Israel—here is a snapshot of how they worked:
   - Deuteronomy 25:17-19—"Don't forget what Amalek did to you on the road after you left Egypt, 18 how he attacked you when you were tired, barely able to put one foot in front of another,

mercilessly cut off your stragglers, and had no regard for God. 19 When GOD, your God, gives you rest from all the enemies that surround you in the inheritance-land GOD, your God, is giving you to possess, you are to wipe the name of Amalek from off the Earth. Don't forget!"

- Amalek opposed the purposes and plans of God by consistently wearying and wearing down the People of God.
- They would strike the Israelites from their rear as they travelled through the wilderness!
- Amalek (the flesh) strives to strike while you are weak and tired—Oh that is why we have such Scriptures—Let the weak say I AM STRONG!
- They struck the weak and the stragglers—in the context of an organisation or local church or group; stragglers would open themselves up to be a target for the Amalekites, and if they got wounded, then they would place pressure on the whole group!
- Very important, Amalek loves to strike out at you when like the Israelites you decide to leave Egypt (we are not speaking of a physical country but a type of the world). Once you consciously decide that you will not submit to the world and the flesh, the enemy seeks to make a "last ditch" effort to get you to change your mind—Hebrews 10:32-36.

"Remember those earlier days after you had received the light, when you endured in a great conflict full of suffering. 33 Sometimes you were publicly exposed to insult and persecution; at other times you stood side by side with those who were so treated. 34 You suffered along with those in prison and joyfully accepted the confiscation of your property, because you knew that you yourselves had better and lasting possessions. 35 So do not throw away your confidence; it will be richly rewarded. 36 You need to persevere so that when you have done the will of God, you will receive what he has promised."

"Remember those early days after you first saw the light? Those were the hard times! Kicked around in public, targets of every kind of abuse—some days it was you, other days your friends. If some friends went to prison, you stuck by them. If some enemies broke in and seized your goods, you let them go with a smile, knowing they couldn't touch your real treasure. Nothing they did bothered you, nothing set you back. So don't throw it all away now. You were sure of yourselves then. It's still a sure thing! But you need to stick it out, staying with God's plan so you'll be there for the promised completion." MSG

7. Amalek's remembrance would be removed from under heaven.
8. God signed the promise with a new revelation of His Name—Jehovah Nissi (Jehovah my Banner).
9. God proclaimed and swore in the spirit realm that He would war with Amalek from generation to generation.

So in the Book of Esther we see the spirit of Amalek rising up to make another attempt in destroying the people of God; this time it is disguised in Haman's hatred towards Mordecai. Haman devised a wicked plan whereby he had the king decree that all the Israelites should bow when in Haman's presence. Mordecai of course wouldn't bow thus incurring the wrath of Haman. Mordecai's refusal to bow netted him a hanging suspended from gallows measuring 80 feet high.

Mordecai

Mordecai was of the tribe of Benjamin, the same as the Apostle Paul. This is very interesting as Paul is considered "the Apostle " of the New Testament Church for all that the Lord used him to accomplish. In essence Mordecai could be seen as an Apostle and Senior Leader of that local church!

Let us for a brief moment look at that name Benjamin:

It means Son of my right hand. However, when Rachel was giving birth to him she named him "son of my sorrows" as she was dying in labour. His father, Jacob renamed him "son of my right hand". Oh this so reflects our Lord Jesus Christ as He was known as the "Man of sorrows"—Isaiah 53:3; and later called the "Man of God's Right Hand"—Revelation 1:17; Psalms 80:17, 89:21; Acts 5:31.

Ben also means *son of* and Jamin means "*fortunate*"; so Benjamin means "son of the fortunate". The tribe of Benjamin was also a warfaring tribe as prophesied by their father Jacob—Genesis 49:27—this speaks so much to the apostolic nature.

Mordecai was the cousin of Esther, and yet he adopted her as his own daughter—Esther 2:7. He thus foreshadows the adoptive work of the Holy Spirit, the Spirit of Adoption—Romans 8:15. He lived to see Esther go through the preparation to meet king Ahasuerus—Esther 2:7-17.

> "And Mordecai had brought up Hadassah, that is, Esther, his uncle's daughter, for she had neither father nor mother. The young woman was lovely and beautiful. When her father and mother died, Mordecai took her as his own daughter. 8 So it was, when the king's command and decree were heard, and when many young women were gathered at Shushan the citadel, under the custody of Hegai, that Esther also was taken to the king's palace, into the care of Hegai the custodian of the women. 9 Now the young woman pleased him, and she obtained his favour; so he readily gave beauty preparations to her, besides her allowance. Then seven choice maidservants were provided for her from the king's palace, and he moved her and her maidservants to the best place in the house of the women. 10 Esther had not revealed her people or family, for Mordecai had charged her not to reveal it. 11 And every day Mordecai paced in front of the court of the women's quarters, to learn of Esther's welfare and what was happening to her. 12 Each young woman's turn came to go in to King Ahasuerus after she had completed twelve months' preparation, according to the regulations for the women, for thus were the days of their preparation apportioned: six months with oil of myrrh, and six months with perfumes and preparations for beautifying women. 13 Thus prepared, each young woman went to the king, and she was given whatever she desired to take with her from the women's quarters to the king's palace. 14 In the evening she went, and in the morning she returned to the second house

of the women, to the custody of Shaashgaz, the king's eunuch who kept the concubines. She would not go in to the king again unless the king delighted in her and called for her by name. 15 Now when the turn came for Esther the daughter of Abihail the uncle of Mordecai, who had taken her as his daughter, to go in to the king, she requested nothing but what Hegai the king's eunuch, the custodian of the women, advised. And Esther obtained favour in the sight of all who saw her. 16 So Esther was taken to King Ahasuerus, into his royal palace, in the tenth month, which is the month of Tebeth, in the seventh year of his reign. 17 The king loved Esther more than all the other women, and she obtained grace and favour in his sight more than all the virgins; so he set the royal crown upon her head and made her queen instead of Vashti."

This is also the work of the Holy Spirit as He prepares the Bride for Christ. Thus, the king upon seeing Esther immediately had favour towards her and requested she come to his palace. The king loved Esther above all the other women. Mordecai's life is a prototype of the Holy Spirit preparing the Church which the Lord will present to Himself—Ephesians 5:27.

Esther

Esther was the daughter of Abihal, whose name meant "father of might" and he was Mordecai's uncle. Her Hebrew name is Hadassah, which means "myrtle". In classic mythology the myrtle shrub was a symbol of heroism and immortality. For the Hebrews, it typified peace and thanksgiving. It was one of the ingredients for the making of the special "anointing oil" that was only to be used by the High Priest. This same oil was to be poured upon the community wherever the Lord found the people dwelling together in unity according to Psalms 133. It was also one of the four kinds of bow branches used for the making of the booths for the Feast of Tabernacles. Myrtle is very fragrant and was used to make wreaths for the heads of nobles. If this isn't a name pregnant with meaning I don't know what is.

The Church, like Esther, is to be brave and of course it is immortal. We, the Church have to live in peace and bring peace. The Church is the Dwelling Place of God—His Tabernacle. It will be crowned as royalty. It is a place where true unity is to be shown forth and experienced—Ephesians 4:11-18! Unity is one of our greatest strengths as a people who share one heart and one mind that is solely focused on God. David asked God to unite his heart. In essence what David was asking God for was to ensure that no other allegiance or distraction would cause him to stray. It is important to realize that we can construct a corporate expression of one heart and one mind for Christ.

> "Also the hand of God was on Judah to give them singleness of heart to obey the command of the king and the leaders, at the word of the Lord." 2 Chronicles 30:12

God is the source of unity and He can only grant it when each member is totally "sold out" to Him. This is why unity is so very powerful. The Lord commands His blessing where there is unity and together as a unified people we can do more than if we were apart. The following Scriptures give us some powerful examples of what unity can accomplish.

> "Five of you shall chase a hundred, and a hundred of you shall put ten thousand to flight; your enemies shall fall by the sword before you." Leviticus 26:8

> "Behold, how good and how pleasant *it is* For brethren to dwell together in unity! 2 *It is like the precious oil* upon the head, Running down on the beard, The beard of Aaron, Running down on the edge of his garments. 3 *It is like the dew of Hermon,* Descending upon the mountains of Zion; *For there the LORD commanded the blessing—Life forevermore."* [Italics added] Psalms 133

Characteristics Of Unity

The Principle

It is dwelling together in unity or when He finds a family, or a marriage or a ministry or a church, and then the promise comes.

Anointing

Precious oil poured on the head down to the end of the garment, thus an anointing will flow from God. This was a special oil and was not to be used on man's flesh, however, God commands it to be used wherever He finds people dwelling in unity. This oil is found in Exodus 30:22-33

Prosperity

The dew of Hermon was higher than Zion, and it was never affected by the prevailing climate of its region. Dew is always used synonymously with blessing, favour, increase, etc—Genesis 27:27-29; Deuteronomy 33:24-29; Proverbs 19:12. It refers to a Blessing of life forever more: this is not just eternal life; this is something that will have generational longevity. This is building something that will become a legacy.

The Anointing Oil

> "Moreover the Lord spoke to Moses, saying: 23 "Also take for yourself quality spices—five hundred shekels of liquid myrrh, half as much sweet-smelling cinnamon (two hundred and fifty shekels), two hundred and fifty shekels of sweet-smelling cane, 24 five hundred shekels of cassia, according to the shekel of the sanctuary, and a hin of olive oil. 25 And you shall make from these a holy anointing oil, an ointment compounded according to the art of the perfumer. It shall be a holy anointing oil. 26 With it you shall anoint the tabernacle of meeting and the ark of the Testimony; 27 the table and all its utensils, the lampstand and its utensils, and the altar of incense; 28 the altar of burnt offering with all its utensils, and the laver and its base. 29 You shall consecrate them, that they may be most holy; whatever touches them must be holy. 30 And you shall anoint Aaron and his sons, and consecrate them, that they may minister to Me

as priests. 31 "And you shall speak to the children of Israel, saying: 'This shall be a holy anointing oil to Me throughout your generations. 32 It shall not be poured on man's flesh; nor shall you make any other like it, according to its composition. It is holy, and it shall be holy to you. 33 Whoever compounds any like it, or whoever puts any of it on an outsider, shall be cut off from his" Exodus 30:22-33

Ingredients Of The Anointing Oil

Myrrh

In Hebrew it means "bitter" or "free" and was taken from the gum of the dwarf tree. It was supposed to flow spontaneously as the tree was cut. Pure Myrrh is bitter to the taste but has a fragrant odour. This speaks of the suffering and the resulting anointed life and ministry we experience—see Mark 15:23; John 19:39; Song of Solomon 3:6, 5:1-17; Matthew 2:11; Psalms 12:6; Esther 2:12; Zephaniah 3:8-9; Philippians 4:8; James 1:27; Revelation 22:1.

Also note that it was used as perfume (Psalms 45:8; Proverbs 7:17; Song of Solomon 3:6), in purification rites for women (Esther 2:12), as a gift for the infant Jesus (Matthew 2:11), and in embalming (signifying death to self and the flesh John 19:39).

Sweet Cinnamon

The Hebrew word for this spice means "fragrance". This spice comes from a small evergreen (constant life) tree that has flowers with a disagreeable odour, yet the spice will improve the flavour of bitter substances (sweetness in suffering). See Psalms 119:103; Song of Solomon 2:3; Ephesians 5:2.

Sweet-smelling Cane or Calamus

In Hebrew this plant's name means, "to stand upright, branch, reed"—Ezekiel 40:3; Isaiah 42:3. It cannot grow in mire—representing the "flesh or sin life"—Isaiah 19:6. This aromatic reed scents the air while growing. When cut down, dried, and powdered, it was used as an ingredient in the richest perfumes—representing the fragrance of Christ in the Believer through times of crushing and shaping—Psalms 68:30.

Cassia

In Hebrew the word Cassia means to, "stoop or bow down, scrape, cleave". This plant has purple flowers (representing royalty) flowers and lives at a very high (heavenly) altitude. This spice was very important as it was also used as incense and to scent garments. In essence, Cassia speaks to Christ's regal character manifested in us as kings and priests unto God—Revelation 1:6. "Cleave"—means to become one—Genesis 32:24-32; Ezekiel 27:19; Psalms 45:8; 2 Samuel 15:19-21; Joshua 23:4; Ruth 1:14-18.

There Were Some Prohibitions Concerning The Anointing Oil:

- It was not to be poured on man's flesh. The oil was for Aaron and his sons (seed) and their spiritual ministry—Psalms 133; 104:15; 23:5.
- It was not to be imitated in any way—for example in the harlot's bed of Proverbs 7:17.
- It was not to be put upon a stranger. The Holy vessels of the Tabernacle are anointed (we, the Believers are now the vessels of God).

In spite of all the restrictions of this oil, whenever the Lord sees "networking" and "unity", He responds by pouring it upon us.

> "Now the multitude of those who believed were of one heart and soul; neither did anyone say that any of the things he possessed was his own, but they had all things in common. 33 And with great power the apostle gave witness to the resurrection of the Lord Jesus. And great grace was upon them all." Acts 4:32-33

We know that since the Book of Acts was written the Church has yet to rise up and experience the signs, wonders, and miracles that occurred in that time period. Why are we not currently in that same dimension of great grace? Since that time we have not been able as a body to walk with the same degree of unity. To have one heart and one mind is to be "*in sync*" with one another, and to "*breathe spiritually*" together as one. As the local church comes together in unity and the

Body of Christ unites we will see miraculous conversions—Acts 2:47, and signs, wonders and miracles being done.

Myrtle

As we saw earlier Esther's name meant Myrtle, and this is also a picture of God's Promised Blessings:

> "Instead of the thorn shall come up the cypress tree, And instead of the brier shall come up the myrtle tree; And it shall be to the LORD for a name, For an everlasting sign that shall not be cut off." Isaiah 53:13

> "The poor and needy seek water, but there is none, Their tongues fail for thirst. I, the LORD, will hear them; I, the God of Israel, will not forsake them. 18 I will open rivers in desolate heights, And fountains in the midst of the valleys; I will make the wilderness a pool of water, And the dry land springs of water. 19 I will plant in the wilderness the cedar and the acacia tree, The myrtle and the oil tree; I will set in the desert the cypress tree and the pine And the box tree together, 20 That they may see and know, And consider and understand together, That the hand of the LORD has done this, And the Holy One of Israel has created it." Isaiah 41:17-20

It was also used to make booths for the Feast of Tabernacles—or the Feast of Booths or Ingathering: This feast consisted of three main elements, which were:

- The Blowing of Trumpets—Leviticus 23:24-25.
- The Day of Atonement—Leviticus 16; 23:27-32.
- The Feast of Tabernacles—Exodus 23:16; Leviticus 23:34-44; Deuteronomy 16:13-15.

Chapter Two

Exploring the Feasts

In order to fully understand the relevance and importance of the Feast of Tabernacles and what it means to the Believer, we need to briefly explore the other Feasts that were celebrated by the Children of Israel and how they relate to us as Born-Again Believers in Jesus Christ. It may seem laborious at the outset, but the revisiting of these portions of Scripture is very necessary as we shall see.

The word for feast in the Hebrew is the word "*moed*" and is translated—a fixed time, appointment, appointed season, festival or feast! For this writing we will use the word season. In Leviticus 23:44 "So Moses declared to the children of Israel the feasts of the LORD."

Declaring the Seasons

Our responsibility/mandate as apostolic-prophetic voices in the earth and/or our specific regions or territories is to declare to the Church and our region the seasons that God has ordained for the Church. For example when Moses died that signalled the end of one season and the beginning of another. It was a very significant time and the Lord God declared "Moses My servant is dead", thus signifying that He was about to raise up a new generation of leadership under Joshua to take the people into the "Promised Land". The Lord declared to Joshua "Moses My servant is DEAD"!

And as was said before, part of the apostolic-prophetic mandate is to declare to God's people the different seasons of the Lord. Now there were three Major Feasts that the Lord instructed Moses to institute—they were Passover, Pentecost and the Feast of Tabernacles; and these were type and shadows of New Testament realities. These were "natural" Feasts or seasons for Israel but very "spiritual" or "prophetic" for the Church!

We have come to the realization of a very basic problem with most church leaders; they are in one season while still living out another season. What do I mean by that? Some are still living in "Passover and Pentecost" when the season has long changed and we are heading into the "Feast of Tabernacles" which is very different from the previous seasons! Another phenomena that we have noticed, is that with every "*New Move*" of God the previous move always persecutes this "*New Move*". We see this today as some of the Pentecostal/Word of Faith/ Charismatic; etc type churches are persecuting this new apostolic move of God!

All these feasts have tremendous Spiritual significance for the New Testament Believer. Let me give you a breakdown of these feasts. The First Feast Was Called Passover!

> "These are the feasts of the LORD, holy convocations which you shall proclaim at their appointed times. 5 On the fourteenth day of the first month at twilight is the LORD's Passover." Leviticus 23:4-5

The Passover

Passover was the first Feast and in typology of the Bible, the number one represents—new beginnings, similar to Salvation, which represents a new beginning. The Feast of the Passover, which is also called the Feast of Unleavened Bread—consisted of three main elements, which were:

- The Passover—Exodus 12:1-23; Leviticus 23:4-5; Deuteronomy 16:1-3.
- The Unleavened Bread—Exodus 12:18, 23:15; Leviticus 23:6-8; Deuteronomy 16:3-4.
- The Sheaf of First-fruits—Leviticus 23:10-14.

This was fulfilled in Jesus who became the Perfect Lamb that was slain and His Blood was applied to our lives saving us from eternal death!

- Jesus is our Passover—1 Corinthians 5:7.
- Jesus is our Unleavened Bread—Matthew 26:17, 26-28; 1 Corinthians 11:23-26.
- Jesus is our Sheaf of Firstfruits—1 Corinthians 15:20-23.

The Bible has a lot to say about [1]*leaven*; however, leaven is first mentioned in Exodus 12:1-20 when the children of Israel were about to depart from Egypt.

> "Now the LORD spoke to Moses and Aaron in the land of Egypt, saying, 2 "This month shall be your beginning of months; it shall be the first month of the year to you. 3 Speak to all the congregation of Israel, saying: 'On the tenth day of this month every man shall take for himself a lamb, according to the house of his father, a lamb for a household. 4 And if the household is too small for the lamb, let him and his neighbour next to his house take it according to the number of the persons; according to each man's need you shall make your count for the lamb. 5 Your lamb shall be without blemish, a male of the first year. You may take it from the sheep or from the goats. 6 Now you shall keep it until the fourteenth day of the same month. Then the whole assembly of the congregation of Israel shall kill it at twilight. 7 And they shall take some of the blood and put it on the two doorposts and on the lintel of the houses where they eat it. 8 Then they shall eat the flesh on that night; roasted in fire,

1 For a more in-depth study on the subject of leaven you can read the author's book titled "Leaven Revealed" ISBN 978-1-77069-108-7. Ordering details at the end of this book.

with unleavened bread and with bitter herbs they shall eat it. 9 Do not eat it raw, nor boiled at all with water, but roasted in fire--its head with its legs and its entrails. 10 You shall let none of it remain until morning, and what remains of it until morning you shall burn with fire. 11 And thus you shall eat it: with a belt on your waist, your sandals on your feet, and your staff in your hand. So you shall eat it in haste. It is the LORD's Passover. 12 For I will pass through the land of Egypt on that night, and will strike all the firstborn in the land of Egypt, both man and beast; and against all the gods of Egypt I will execute judgment: I am the LORD. 13 Now the blood shall be a sign for you on the houses where you are. And when I see the blood, I will pass over you; and the plague shall not be on you to destroy you when I strike the land of Egypt. 14 So this day shall be to you a memorial; and you shall keep it as a feast to the LORD throughout your generations. You shall keep it as a feast by an everlasting ordinance. 15 Seven days you shall eat unleavened bread. On the first day you shall remove leaven from your houses. For whoever eats leavened bread from the first day until the seventh day, that person shall be cut off from Israel. 16 On the first day there shall be a holy convocation, and on the seventh day there shall be a holy convocation for you. No manner of work shall be done on them; but that which everyone must eat--that only may be prepared by you. 17 So you shall observe the Feast of Unleavened Bread, for on this same day I will have brought your armies out of the land of Egypt. Therefore you shall observe this day throughout your generations as an everlasting ordinance. 18 In the first month, on the fourteenth day of the month at evening, you shall eat unleavened bread, until the twenty-first day of the month at evening. 19 For seven days no leaven shall be found in your houses, since whoever eats what is leavened, that same person shall be cut off from the congregation of Israel, whether he is a stranger or a native of the land. 20 You shall eat nothing leavened; in all your dwellings you shall eat unleavened bread."

In the New Testament there are at least five types of "*leaven*" spoken about with their corrupting influences and it would do well for us to briefly explore them to ensure that we keep this Feast accurate in our lives!

1. The leaven of the Pharisees—Matthew 16:6-11; Luke 12:1.
2. The leaven of the Sadducees—Matthew 16:1-12; Matthew 22:23.
3. The leaven of the Corinthians—1 Corinthians 5:1-8.
4. The leaven of the Galatians—Galatians 5:1-9.
5. The leaven of Herod or the Herodians—Mark 8:15.

We also saw this season begin through the Protestant Reformation that began with Martin Luther—Luther's writings emphasized the Blood of Jesus Christ, Justification by Faith, etc.

Going a bit deeper into this first Feast we observe that on the 15th day of Nissan, (the first month of the Hebrew calendar) there was the institution of the Unleavened Bread, which represents Sanctification. This was paralleled when the Lord began using the Methodist and Wesleyans Holiness Churches in the 18th Century to preach Holiness and Sanctification, thereby helping with the removal of leaven (sin) from our lives and homes.

In the study of Scriptures, there is a principle, which is known as the "*first mention principle*" or "*law of first mention*". This is a principle by which the interpretation of any verse is aided by considering the first time its subject appears in Scripture. In general, the first time a principle is mentioned in Scripture, it carries with it a meaning, which will be consistent throughout the entire Bible. So as we study leaven from the New Testament perspective we want to keep this in mind; the Lord wants *leaven* eradicated from our lives and ministries!

The Spiritual Significance of Leaven in The New Testament

The Apostle Paul writing by the Holy Spirit puts it succinctly as he communicated to both the Corinthian and Galatians churches. In the Corinthian church he had to deal with sexual impurity and in the Galatians church he had to deal with Judaism and bondage to the Law.

"Your glorying is not good. Do you not know that a little leaven leavens the whole lump? 7 Therefore purge out the old leaven, that you may be a new lump, since you truly are unleavened. For indeed Christ, our Passover, was sacrificed for us. 8 Therefore let us keep the feast, not with old leaven, nor with the leaven of malice and wickedness, but with the unleavened bread of sincerity and truth." 1 Corinthians 5:6-8

"Stand fast therefore in the liberty by which Christ has made us free, and do not be entangled again with a yoke of bondage. 2 Indeed I, Paul, say to you that if you become circumcised, Christ will profit you nothing. 3 And I testify again to every man who becomes circumcised that he is a debtor to keep the whole law. 4 You have become estranged from Christ, you who attempt to be justified by law; you have fallen from grace. 5 For we through the Spirit eagerly wait for the hope of righteousness by faith. 6 For in Christ Jesus neither circumcision nor uncircumcision avails anything, but faith working through love. 7 You ran well. Who hindered you from obeying the truth? 8 This persuasion does not come from Him who calls you. 9 A little leaven leavens the whole lump." Galatians 5: 1-9

How Do We Remain Free Of Leaven?

We need to go back to the origins of this command and see what happened—keeping in mind the principle called the "Law of First Mention".

- The Passover was established as a symbol of the Lord spearing us from death because of the Blood of the Lamb (Jesus Christ) on the doorposts of our lives.
- The children of Israel left Egypt (a type of the world) in haste and as a result they did not have time for their bread (lives) to contain leaven—Exodus 12:39.
- So it is with us as long as we keep pressing on in the things of God and keep ourselves from the corrupting influences of the world, the flesh and the devil, we will be free of leaven (sin and corruption).

I tell you if we begin to lose sight of what the Lord has called us to, or if we begin to lose sight of the Lord's Glory and the nature of Jesus Christ, before long we will become filled with the leaven of malice and wickedness.

- Nature teaches us that there is only one way to keep a stream of water clean and pure?—That is to keep it flowing!
- Many times leaven seeps into our lives when we think that we have attained a significant position because of some new revelation or some knowledge of the Word of God. That's when we begin to think that we are like God and that we are better than everyone else, thus causing leaven to step into our lives. It is the very same temptation Eve and Adam found themselves in, which caused them to be cast out of the Garden of God. The Bible declares this in 1 Corinthians 8:1b-3 "We know that we all have knowledge. Knowledge puffs up, but love edifies. 2 And if anyone thinks that he knows anything, he knows nothing yet as he ought to know. 3 But if anyone loves God, this one is known by Him." This is why *revelation received must be progressive, truth is progressive—we can only be fully complete in all things when we receive our New Bodies from Heaven*!

[2]The Leaven Of The Pharisees

Leaven of the Pharisees—it's a curious phrase. Why did Jesus Christ feel compelled to warn His disciples to avoid it? Would you recognize this "state of leavening" if you saw it today? Answers to these questions are very important. However, the scope of this writing is not intended to go into that depth. For more on this and the other leavens spoken of in Scripture you can secure a copy of the author's book—"Leaven Revealed"—ordering details at the end of this book!

What is this "leaven of the Pharisees"? You will find a direct answer in Matthew 16:6-11; Luke 12:1.

> "Then Jesus said to them, "Take heed and beware of the leaven of the Pharisees and the Sadducees." 7 And they reasoned among themselves, saying, "It is because we have taken no

---

2 For more on the subject of leaven you can read the author's book titled "Leaven Revealed" ISBN 978-1-77069-108-7. Ordering details at the end of this book.

bread." 8 But Jesus, being aware of it, said to them, "O you of little faith, why do you reason among yourselves because you have brought no bread? 9 Do you not yet understand, or remember the five loaves of the five thousand and how many baskets you took up? 10 Nor the seven loaves of the four thousand and how many large baskets you took up? 11 How is it you do not understand that I did not speak to you concerning bread?--but to beware of the leaven of the Pharisees and Sadducees." 12 Then they understood that He did not tell them to beware of the leaven of bread, but of the doctrine of the Pharisees and Sadducees." Matthew 16:6-11

"In the meantime, when an innumerable multitude of people had gathered together, so that they trampled one another, He began to say to His disciples first of all, "Beware of the *leaven of the Pharisees, which is hypocrisy*." [Italics added] Luke 12:1

Hypocrisy

This comes from the Greek word "hupokrisis" and is rendered—acting under a feigned part, i.e. (figuratively) deceit ("hypocrisy"): also "a reply, an answer" "play-acting," as the actors spoke in dialogue; hence, "pretence, hypocrisy"; it is translated "hypocrisy"—*pretending to act from one motive, whereas another motive really inspires the act.* For examples where this word is used you can read the following passages from the Scriptures: Matthew 23; Mark 12:15; Luke 12:1; 1 Timothy 4:1-2. In 1 Peter 2:1-3 "Therefore, laying aside all malice, all guile, hypocrisy, envy, and all evil speaking, 2 as newborn babes, desire the pure milk of the word, that you may grow thereby, 3 if indeed you have tasted that the Lord is gracious." Here we see the Lord stipulating that one of the criterions for receiving the Pure Word of God is that we must lay aside or put away any form of hypocrisy.

In Galatians 2 we read of a major dissention between the Apostles Paul and Peter, because of Peter's hypocrisy when in the company of the Jews. That hypocrisy threatened to destroy their relationship; hence the Apostle Paul had to effectively deal with it by confronting Peter and taking up the matter with him.

There is one other Greek word "anupokritos", which is rendered "without hypocrisy," and the Scriptures encourage us to be in sync with that word. In James 3:13-18, we are encouraged to seek the Lord for His Wisdom, the one that comes from above and is without hypocrisy. And in Romans 12:9-21 we are encouraged to let the foundation of our lives and ministry be that of "*love without hypocrisy*".

> "Who is wise and understanding among you? Let him show by good conduct that his works are done in the meekness of wisdom. 14 But if you have bitter envy and self-seeking in your hearts, do not boast and lie against the truth. 15 This wisdom does not descend from above, but is earthly, sensual, demonic. 16 For where envy and self-seeking exist, confusion and every evil thing are there. 17 But the wisdom that is from above is first pure, then peaceable, gentle, willing to yield, full of mercy and good fruits, without partiality and without hypocrisy. 18 Now the fruit of righteousness is sown in peace by those who make peace." James 3:13-18

> "Let love be without hypocrisy. Abhor what is evil. Cling to what is good. 10 Be kindly affectionate to one another with brotherly love, in honour giving preference to one another; 11 not lagging in diligence, fervent in spirit, serving the Lord; 12 rejoicing in hope, patient in tribulation, continuing steadfastly in prayer; 13 distributing to the needs of the saints, given to hospitality. 14 Bless those who persecute you; bless and do not curse. 15 Rejoice with those who rejoice, and weep with those who weep. 16 Be of the same mind toward one another. Do not set your mind on high things, but associate with the humble. Do not be wise in your own opinion. 17 Repay no one evil for evil. Have regard for good things in the sight of all men. 18 If it is possible, as much as depends on you, live peaceably with all men. 19 Beloved, do not avenge yourselves, but rather give place to wrath; for it is written, "Vengeance is Mine, I will repay," says the Lord. 20 Therefore "If your enemy is hungry, feed him; If he is thirsty, give him a

drink; For in so doing you will heap coals of fire on his head."
21 Do not be overcome by evil, but overcome evil with good."

[3]The Leaven Of The Sadducees

The Sadducees were another priestly group and some Christians probably lump them together with the Pharisees as they are often mentioned together in the Bible. But the Sadducees were very different from the Pharisees as they were descendants of Aaron and associated with the leadership of the Temple in Jerusalem. Of note, during Jesus Christ's time on earth the religious/political group of the Sadducees was known for their liberalism. They were very aristocratic and tended to be very wealthy and held very powerful positions, such as that of high priest.

The Sadducees held fast to the written Word of God—especially the Pentateuch, which is comprised of Genesis through Deuteronomy and is also known as the Five Books of Moses. However, due to their extremely political bias they tended to compromise Scripture and adopted some erroneous doctrinal practices and beliefs. As a matter of fact these religious zealots of the day were the ones who with the Pharisees plotted to crucify Jesus Christ when their authority was severely being threatened by His teachings.

"Then the Pharisees and Sadducees came, and testing Him
asked that He would show them a sign from heaven. 2 He
answered and said to them, "When it is evening you say, 'It
will be fair weather, for the sky is red'; 3 and in the morning, 'It
will be foul weather today, for the sky is red and threatening.'
Hypocrites! You know how to discern the face of the sky, but
you cannot discern the signs of the times. 4 A wicked and
adulterous generation seeks after a sign, and no sign shall be
given to it except the sign of the prophet Jonah." And He left
them and departed. 5 Now when His disciples had come to
the other side, they had forgotten to take bread. 6 Then Jesus
said to them, "Take heed and beware of the leaven of the
Pharisees and the Sadducees." 7 And they reasoned among

3 For more on the subject of leaven you can read the author's book titled "Leaven Revealed" ISBN 978-1-77069-108-7. Ordering details at the end of this book.

> themselves, saying, "It is because we have taken no bread." 8 But Jesus, being aware of it, said to them, "O you of little faith, why do you reason among yourselves because you have brought no bread? 9 Do you not yet understand, or remember the five loaves of the five thousand and how many baskets you took up? 10 Nor the seven loaves of the four thousand and how many large baskets you took up? 11 How is it you do not understand that I did not speak to you concerning bread?--but to beware of the leaven of the Pharisees and Sadducees." 12 Then they understood that He did not tell them to beware of the leaven of bread, but of the doctrine of the Pharisees and Sadducees. Matthew 16:1-12

> "The same day the Sadducees, *who say there is no resurrection*, came to Him and asked Him…" [Italics added] Matthew 22:23

The Sadducees did not believe in the resurrection of the dead or the immortality of the soul. Neither did they believe in rewards nor in punishments handed out after death, as in the doctrines of Heaven and hell. Acts 23:6-8 indicates that they did not believe in angels or spirits, either.

> "But when Paul perceived that one part were Sadducees and the other Pharisees, he cried out in the council, "Men and brethren, I am a Pharisee, the son of a Pharisee; concerning the hope and resurrection of the dead I am being judged!" 7 And when he had said this, a dissension arose between the Pharisees and the Sadducees; and the assembly was divided. 8 For Sadducees say that there is no resurrection--and no angel or spirit; but the Pharisees confess both."

The Sadducees were legalists and held their people in bondage to the Law. So then the leaven of the Sadducees is "legalism and unbelief in the Resurrection".

[4]The Leaven Of The Corinthians

In order to fully understand the leaven of the Corinthians, it would be very beneficial if we first understand a bit about the city and its origins.

[5]Corinth, or Korinth (Κόρινθος) is a Greek city on the Isthmus of Corinth, the narrow stretch of land that joins the Peloponnesus to the mainland of Greece. To the west of the isthmus lies the Gulf of Corinth. Like its ancient predecessor, modern Corinth is the center of commerce between northern and southern Greece. Today, it has a population of about 30,000, far less than the estimated 500,000 in the days that Apostle Paul lived and ministered there.

The Corinth of Apostle Paul's day was relatively new. The old Corinth (which was famous and powerful in the days of the Peloponnesian War) was burned in 146 BC by the Roman proconsul, L. Mummius. Because it was a city devoted to the gods, a hundred years were required to pass before the city could be rebuilt. In 46 BC, Julius Caesar rebuilt the city, populated it with a colony of veterans and free men, and named it Julia Corinthus. And soon, it became a very important commercial center.

With its new found reputation as being a prominent center of commerce in the Mediterranean world, it swiftly became a place for all sorts of vice. An example of its immorality was found in the temple of Venus (Aphrodite), which hosted 1000 priestesses dedicated to prostitution in the name of religion. The city became so well known for such immorality that the very name was made into a verb. To "corinthianize" literally meant to go to bed with a prostitute.

The Corinthian church was made up of a core of Jewish Believers but many of its members were saved out of this pagan background, bringing with them their pagan practices in the newly established church. Apostle Paul arrived in Corinth in AD 51 to preach the Word of God. While there he established a church and remained in the church for 18 months to bring the Word of God to them—Acts 18:1-18. A couple of years after leaving he received a letter from the church that explained some problems the church was having and asked

---

4 For more on the subject of leaven you can read the author's book titled "Leaven Revealed" ISBN 978-1-77069-108-7. Ordering details at the end of this book.

5 Adapted from an article at http://www.mlahanas.de/Greece/Regions/Geraneia.html

for guidance—1 Corinthians 7:1. He also received some additional information from an independent family (Chloe's household) in the church that further explained the problems the church was facing—1 Corinthians 1:11.

While the actual reference to leaven is found in the following passage of Scripture, its debilitating effects are plastered throughout the Apostle Paul's letter to the Corinthian Saints.

> "It is actually reported that there is *sexual immorality* among you, and such *sexual immorality* as is not even named among the Gentiles--that a man has his father's wife! 2 And you are puffed up, and have not rather mourned, that he who has done this deed might be taken away from among you. 3 For I indeed, as absent in body but present in spirit, have already judged [as though I were present] him who has so done this deed. 4 In the name of our Lord Jesus Christ, when you are gathered together, along with my spirit, with the power of our Lord Jesus Christ, 5 deliver such a one to satan for the destruction of the flesh, that his spirit may be saved in the day of the Lord Jesus. 6 Your glorying is not good. Do you not know that a little leaven leavens the whole lump? 7 Therefore purge out the old leaven, that you may be a new lump, since you truly are unleavened. For indeed Christ, our Passover, was sacrificed for us. 8 Therefore let us keep the feast, not with old leaven, nor with *the leaven of malice and wickedness*, but with the unleavened bread of sincerity and truth." [Italics added] 1 Corinthians 5:1-8

As such the leaven of the Corinthians is sexual immorality, malice and wickedness.

[6]The Leaven Of The Galatians

The territory in modern central Turkey known as Galatia was an oddity in the Eastern world. It was originally home of the ancient civilization of the Hittites, but came to be occupied by Gallic Celts

6 For more on the subject of leaven you can read the author's book titled "Leaven Revealed" ISBN 978-1-77069-108-7. Ordering details at the end of this book.

in the 3rd century BC, hence Galatia, or "Gallia of the East." Galatia also became an early stronghold for the Christian church. The Apostle Paul visited the province around AD 55 and wrote his Epistle to the Galatians. The Celts apparently took to his teaching in earnest and the early church spread and flourished.

However, it was not long after the establishment of a strong church in Galatia that major problems surfaced due to erroneous doctrine that was introduced with the intent of completely destroying the church. Because of this chaotic influence of false doctrine permeating the church, the Apostle Paul wrote a very significant and serious letter to the Galatians. The entire Epistle was written to counteract the leavening influence of a few Judaizers (Believers who mixed the rituals of Judaism with their Christian faith) who had come amongst the Galatians, and were endeavouring to persuade them that in order to be *perfect* Christians it was necessary to be circumcised and observe the Law of Moses.

In order to effectively refute the debilitating effect of their leaven, Apostle Paul began his apologetic first by defending his Apostolic authority by proving that God called him and imparted the truth of the Gospel to him by means of a direct revelation. Secondly, Apostle Paul aggressively exposed the leaven of the Judaizers. He knew it was incumbent on him to expose the leaven and its errors that were leading the Galatians astray.

> "Stand fast therefore in the liberty by which Christ has made us free, and do not be entangled again with a yoke of bondage. 2 Indeed I, Paul, say to you that if you become circumcised, Christ will profit you nothing. 3 And I testify again to every man who becomes circumcised that he is a debtor to keep the whole law. 4 You have become estranged from Christ, you who attempt to be justified by law; you have fallen from grace. 5 For we through the Spirit eagerly wait for the hope of righteousness by faith. 6 For in Christ Jesus neither circumcision nor uncircumcision avails anything, but faith working through love. 7 You ran well. Who hindered you from obeying the truth? 8 This persuasion does not come from Him who calls you. 9 A little leaven leavens the whole lump." Galatians 5:1-9

The leaven of the Galatians was folly, legalism or works to be saved rather than the Grace of God. It also represents religiosity, walking in the flesh rather than walking in the Spirit, being bewitched and turning away from "Present Truth[7]"—you can read Galatians 1:6-10; Galatians 3:1-3; Galatians 4:9-11; Galatians 5:13-26.

[8]The Leaven Of Herod

The leaven of Herod is not usually a separate subject of study or discussion when referencing the effect of leaven as usually they get lumped together—Mark 8:15 speaks of the leaven of the Pharisees and the leaven of Herod. But we do well to explore the impact of this statement. Herod was the tetrarch of Galilee, the son of Herod the Great and he contributed greatly to the corrupt leaven weaving its way into Jewish society.

Under the Roman system of government the territory of Galilee was under the joint rule of four rulers. Herod like his father before him, was ruthless in his rule and interestingly enough, he was the only monarch who reigned with a watered-down lineage. He was Jewish only on his father's side and the lineage of his mother was that of a Samaritan. This in itself placed Herod in a negative light as the Samaritans were despised by ordinary Jews. A Jew believed that he could become contaminated by passing through Samaritan territory, and therefore would detour to avoid such a trek.

Likewise, the Samaritans often taunted the Jews. They rejected all of the Old Testament except the Pentateuch, and they claimed to have an older copy of the Book, therefore a more precise guidebook which allowed them to boast that they could observe the precepts better. According to John 4:12, the Jews repaid the Samaritans with hatred. They rejected the Samaritan copy of the law and publicly denounced that Samaritans were of any Jewish birth—John 4:12.

Herod fought a battle within himself and in a time where power and position were in direct alignment with keeping the bloodlines pure, Herod had to show his strength and power by keeping his subjects at

---

7 For a more comprehensive understanding of "Present Truth" see the author's book – "Five Pillars of the Apostolic" ISBN 0-9686896-0-4. Ordering details at the end of this book.

8 For more on the subject of leaven you can read the author's book titled "Leaven Revealed" ISBN 978-1-77069-108-7. Ordering details at the end of this book.

bay. This was certainly evident in the corruption of his rule from these glimpses into his life from Scripture.

Rule in the Roman system was usually achieved by those who gained (by bribes, or service) the favour of Caesar. The whole system was corrupt. It was not the office of the king that was corrupt in and of itself but rather, the warnings of Jesus Christ about the leaven of Herod pointed to the process of gaining this office which was corrupt as it could be gotten by bribes. It had a strong influence on Israel as a society, without thought of integrity or transparency.

As far as the Herodians were concerned, nothing was actually sinful; and as long as you 'believed' in God, everything was okay. In fact, according to historians, the Herodians were an influential religious and political group comprised of Jews who catered to Herod, accepted the Roman way of life, and were favourable toward Greek customs and passions. In other words, these were the supposedly 'enlightened' Jews who claimed they had faith in God, yet curried political and social favour by not imposing their beliefs on others. The Herodians were the "*inclusive church*", the "*politically correct church*", and indeed the "*cool church*" of their day.

In their own demented way, the Herodians actually thought that by embracing the world's system and values and incorporating them into their Jewish 'faith', they could not only draw more followers into their 'denomination', but be able to preserve it as well. This colossal deception led to the Herodians becoming the ultimate compromisers. As a result, rather than being a force for good in their communities they fostered a culture of perverse laws and ungodly practices, and these self-centred man-pleasers instead became agents of and to the antichrist spirit.

Today, in their desire to make God's Word more "socially acceptable" many so-called ministers are presenting a form of Herodianism under the guise of Christianity. For instance, in a current movement known as the "Emergent Church", many of its leaders are now questioning the timeless and fundamental doctrines of our Christian faith. Doctrines such as the reality of hell, the call to holiness, and the Deity of Jesus Christ just to name a few.

Staying true to form, these modern-day Herodian leaders also refuse to address sin, while proclaiming a gospel of 'grace' that denies the need for repentance. Like their predecessors, these self-centred man-pleasers seek only to increase their numbers by promoting a hedonistic, non-judgmental worldview rather than a Christ-centred Biblical one. They shamefully and inaccurately present Jesus as an all-inclusive god who has no boundaries, no distinct form of holiness and no absolute truth.

> "Then He charged them, saying, "Take heed, beware of the leaven of the Pharisees and the leaven of Herod." Mark 8:15

> "Now it happened that He went through the grainfields on the Sabbath; and as they went His disciples began to pluck the heads of grain. 24 And the Pharisees said to Him, "Look, why do they do what is not lawful on the Sabbath?" 25 But He said to them, "Have you never read what David did when he was in need and hungry, he and those with him: 26 how he went into the house of God in the days of Abiathar the high priest, and ate the showbread, which is not lawful to eat, except for the priests, and also gave some to those who were with him?" 27 And He said to them, "The Sabbath was made for man, and not man for the Sabbath. 28 Therefore the Son of Man is also Lord of the Sabbath. Mark 3:1 And He entered the synagogue again, and a man was there who had a withered hand. 2 So they watched Him closely, whether He would heal him on the Sabbath, so that they might accuse Him. 3 And He said to the man who had the withered hand, "Step forward." 4 Then He said to them, "Is it lawful on the Sabbath to do good or to do evil, to save life or to kill?" But they kept silent. 5 And when He had looked around at them with anger, being grieved by the hardness of their hearts, He said to the man, "Stretch out your hand." And he stretched it out, and his hand was restored as whole as the other. 6 Then the Pharisees went out and immediately plotted with the Herodians against Him, how they might destroy Him". Mark 2:23-3:6

> "Then the Pharisees went and plotted how they might entangle Him in His talk. 16 And they sent to Him their disciples with the

> Herodians, saying, "Teacher, we know that You are true, and teach the way of God in truth; nor do You care about anyone, for You do not regard the person of men. 17 Tell us, therefore, what do You think? Is it lawful to pay taxes to Caesar, or not?"
> 18 But Jesus perceived their wickedness, and said, "Why do you test Me, you hypocrites? 19 Show Me the tax money." So they brought Him a denarius. 20 And He said to them, "Whose image and inscription is this?" 21 They said to Him, "Caesar's." And He said to them, "Render therefore to Caesar the things that are Caesar's, and to God the things that are God's." 22 When they had heard these words, they marvelled, and left Him and went their way." Matthew 22:15-22

The leaven of Herod was malice and political guile—Herod used his political office to enforce his way and the Jews played up to his system to get rid of Jesus. Jesus warns against religious politics in the Church. Some, who seek to have control over others by manipulation, use this tactic. This also happens when people begin to play up to men to gain an advantage. Also in some church structures there is the process of voting to elect a Pastor to lead the church. If the chosen Pastor does not adhere to what the members think he should or should not do, then the whole process of voting and manipulation is employed to remove the Pastor or anyone they do not like. It is sad when the *leaven of Herod* enters a church or ministry.

Earthly politics within the Church is one the most deceptive and dangerous realms that needs to be effectively dealt with. Hear me "*church politics*" is a known disease that cripples the immune system of the "Body".

One of the things that I have learnt over the course of my Christian experience is this: quite often the person that you can't stand, or who may rub you the wrong way, is the person the Lord has ordained to sharpen and improve your life. For some of you reading this book it may be your current leader, your wife, your husband, a brother or sister in the church that you are attending. It may even be your boss at work or even your co-worker. Whoever it might be, allow the Lord by His Spirit to unearth your treasure as it is of a great price for someone else!

The Feast of Pentecost/Feast of Weeks/Sheaf of Firstfruits

The third component of the Passover was the Feast of Pentecost or Weeks or the Sheaf of Firstfruits. Do remember that all these Feasts of the Old Testament were fulfilled in Jesus Christ who became the Perfect Lamb that was slain. His Blood was applied to our lives, and we became a New Creation as Believers in Him, thus saving us from eternal death! Jesus Christ is our Sheaf of Firstfruits!

> "But Christ has indeed been raised from the dead, the first-fruits of those who have fallen asleep. 21 For since death came through a man, the resurrection of the dead comes also through a man. 22 For as in Adam all die, so in Christ all will be made alive. 23 But each in his own turn: Christ, the first-fruits; then, when he comes, those who belong to him." 1 Corinthians 15:20-23

> "And the Feast of Harvest, the firstfruits of your labours which you have sown in the field; and the Feast of Ingathering at the end of the year, when you have gathered in the fruit of your labours from the field." Exodus 23:16

> "And you shall count for yourselves from the day after the Sabbath, from the day that you brought the sheaf of the wave offering: seven Sabbaths shall be completed. 16 Count *fifty days* to the day after the seventh Sabbath; then you shall offer a new grain offering to the LORD. 17 You shall bring from your dwellings two wave loaves of two-tenths of an ephah. They shall be of fine flour; they shall be baked with leaven. They are the firstfruits to the LORD. 18 And you shall offer with the bread seven lambs of the first year, without blemish, one young bull, and two rams. They shall be as a burnt offering to the LORD, with their grain offering and their drink offerings, an offering made by fire for a sweet aroma to the LORD. 19 Then you shall sacrifice one kid of the goats as a sin offering, and two male lambs of the first year as a sacrifice of a peace offering. 20 The priest shall wave them with the bread of the firstfruits as a

wave offering before the LORD, with the two lambs. They shall be holy to the LORD for the priest. 21 And you shall proclaim on the same day that it is a holy convocation to you. You shall do no customary work on it. It shall be a statute forever in all your dwellings throughout your generations." [Italics added] Leviticus 23:15-21

"You shall count seven weeks for yourself; begin to count the seven weeks from the time you begin to put the sickle to the grain. 10 Then you shall keep the Feast of Weeks to the LORD your God with the tribute of a freewill offering from your hand, which you shall give as the LORD your God blesses you. 11 You shall rejoice before the LORD your God, you and your son and your daughter, your male servant and your female servant, the Levite who is within your gates, the stranger and the fatherless and the widow who are among you, at the place where the LORD your God chooses to make His name abide. 12 And you shall remember that you were a slave in Egypt, and you shall be careful to observe these statutes." Deuteronomy 16:9-12

Fulfilled in the New Testament Believer

"Now when the Day of Pentecost had fully come, they were all with one accord in one place. 2 And suddenly there came a sound from heaven, as of a rushing mighty wind, and it filled the whole house where they were sitting. 3 Then there appeared to them divided tongues, as of fire, and one sat upon each of them. 4 And they were all filled with the Holy Spirit and began to speak with other tongues, as the Spirit gave them utterance." Acts 2:1-4

This Feast was fulfilled in the New Testament on the Day of Pentecost and is revisited every time someone is baptized in the Holy Spirit. As we just read in Leviticus 23:15-16 God told Moses to count seven Sabbaths which represents forty-nine days, and the day after that, on the fiftieth day the Feast of Pentecost was to be instituted. Fifty represents the number for Pentecost.

This experience continued in the Church for Centuries, but was lost during the period known as the Dark Ages, during this period the Church of Jesus Christ went underground. When that happened we then saw the rise of the Roman Catholic Church system. It was not until 1501 the Roman Catholic Priest named [9]Martin Luther rose up by the Spirit of God and condemned that system for their indulgences and error. From that period in time is when the Reformation of the Church began. Much was restored during the many years of this Reformation. However, it was not until the turn of the Twentieth Century that this great Feast of Pentecost was restored to the Church through what is now referred to as the great Pentecostal Outpouring. That Outpouring gave birth to the great Pentecostal Movement! Thank God for this truth being restored as Believers are still experiencing Pentecost, by being baptized in the Holy Spirit. After the Feast of Pentecost, the Israelites were to celebrate the third and final Feast, which was the Feast of Tabernacles, which is discussed in the following chapter!

9 For more on this see the chapter five ["Present Truth"] of this book.

Chapter Three

Feasts of Tabernacles: A Closer Look

The third feast that Moses was told to introduce was the Feast of Tabernacles, which is also known as the Feast of the Seventh Month. Seven is the number of Perfection or Completion; and the Feast of Tabernacles takes place in the seventh month. The Lord began to show me that the Church could never be perfected with a Passover and Pentecostal Anointing! It takes the Feast of Tabernacles Anointing to bring the Church to completion! Each season that God brings the Church through is designed to equip us for the next move of God! Passover prepared us for Pentecost and Pentecost prepared us for the Feast of Tabernacles!

In the New Testament reality, this move of God is to bring the Church to maturity and this is the vision of the apostolic—to bring God's people to perfection!

The Feast of Tabernacles/Feast of Booths/Ingathering

This Feast consisted of three main elements, which were:

- The Blowing of Trumpets—Leviticus 23:24-25.
- The Day of Atonement—Leviticus 16; 23:27-32.
- The Feast of Tabernacles—Exodus 23:16; Leviticus 23:34-44; Deuteronomy 16:13-15.

The Blowing of Trumpets

> "Speak to the children of Israel, saying: 'In the seventh month, on the first day of the month, you shall have a Sabbath-rest, a memorial of blowing of trumpets, a holy convocation. 25 You shall do no customary work on it; and you shall offer an offering made by fire to the LORD.'" Leviticus 23:24-25

Blowing of Trumpets represents the delivering of a Message and to adhere to this, let us explore and establish this in the Word of God! Trumpets are mentioned sixty times in the Bible and they all indicate a Message, to be heeded, here are a few references: The first time it is mentioned is in Exodus 19:13.

> "Not a hand shall touch him, but he shall surely be stoned or shot *with an arrow;* whether man or beast, he shall not live.' When the trumpet sounds long, they shall come near the mountain."

Joshua with the Walls of Jericho

> "It shall come to pass, when they make a long *blast* with the ram's horn, *and* when you hear the sound of the trumpet, that all the people shall shout with a great shout; then the wall of the city will fall down flat. And the people shall go up every man straight before him." Joshua 6:5

Nehemiah in rebuilding the Walls

> "Every one of the builders had his sword girded at his side as he built. And the one who sounded the trumpet *was* beside me. 19 Then I said to the nobles, the rulers, and the rest of the people, "The work *is* great and extensive, and we are separated far from one another on the wall. 20 Wherever you hear the sound of the trumpet, rally to us there. Our God will fight for us." Nehemiah 4:18-20

> "Again the word of the LORD came to me, saying, 2 "Son of man, speak to the children of your people, and say to them:

'When I bring the sword upon a land, and the people of the land take a man from their territory and make him their watchman, 3 when he sees the sword coming upon the land, if he blows the trumpet and warns the people, 4 then whoever hears the sound of the trumpet and does not take warning, if the sword comes and takes him away, his blood shall be on his *own* head. 5 He heard the sound of the trumpet, but did not take warning; his blood shall be upon himself. But he who takes warning will save his life. 6 But if the watchman sees the sword coming and does not blow the trumpet, and the people are not warned, and the sword comes and takes *any* person from among them, he is taken away in his iniquity; but his blood I will require at the watchman's hand.'" Ezekiel 33:1-6

"Even things without life, whether flute or harp, when they make a sound, unless they make a distinction in the sounds, how will it be known what is piped or played? 8 For if the trumpet makes an uncertain sound, who will prepare for battle? 9 So likewise you, unless you utter by the tongue words easy to understand, how will it be known what is spoken? For you will be speaking into the air." 1 Corinthians 14:7-9

"After these things I looked, and behold, a door standing open in heaven. And the first voice which I heard was like a trumpet speaking with me, saying, "Come up here, and I will show you things which must take place after this." Revelation 4:1

From these references we have established the fact that the Blowing of Trumpets represents a Message being delivered and the preparations for the Feast of Tabernacles begins with the Blowing of Trumpets!

The Significance Of Blowing Trumpets

We get the clearest picture of the significance of the Blowing of Trumpets, during the reign of Moses when the Lord commanded it to be done—Numbers 10:1-10.

> "And the LORD spoke to Moses, saying: 2 "Make two silver trumpets for yourself; you shall make them of hammered work; you shall use them *for calling the congregation* and for directing the movement of the camps. 3 *When they blow both of them, all the congregation shall gather* before you at the door of the tabernacle of meeting. 4 But if they blow *only* one, then the leaders, the heads of the divisions of Israel, shall gather to you. 5 When you sound the advance, the camps that lie on the east side shall then begin their journey. 6 When you sound the advance the second time, then the camps that lie on the south side shall begin their journey; they shall sound the call for them to begin their journeys. 7 And *when the assembly is to be gathered together, you shall blow*, but not sound the advance. 8 The sons of Aaron, the priests, shall blow the trumpets; and these shall be to you as an ordinance forever throughout your generations. 9 "When you go to war in your land against the enemy who oppresses you, then you shall sound an alarm with the trumpets, and you will be remembered before the LORD your God, and you will be saved from your enemies. 10 Also in the day of your gladness, in your appointed feasts, and at the beginning of your months, you shall blow the trumpets over your burnt offerings and over the sacrifices of your peace offerings; and they shall be a memorial for you before your God: I *am* the LORD your God."
> [Italics added]

Calling The Assembly

Verse 2 "Make two silver trumpets for yourself; you shall make them of hammered work; you shall use them for calling the congregation and for directing the movement of the camps."—What does that signify to us today? Well once again the Lord is raising up a John the Baptist ministry to declare the Day of the Lord. There must be the sounding or trumpeting of a clear message in this hour, calling the Church to order, in preparation for the Lord's final return. Let us explore the ministry of John the Baptist through present truth lenses. In the Book of Malachi, which was the last documented speaking of God until the birth of Jesus over Four Hundred years later, we see God placing great emphasis on purity and righteousness. All this cleansing was to take place before the coming of Jesus and it was two fold in nature. While we know that John the Baptist fulfilled the role of being the forerunner to Jesus (*for he came in the spirit and power of Elijah*), we also know that there is a dimension to the fulfilment of that prophetic word which is still to come. The following passage of Scripture will assist in bringing greater clarity to this—Matthew 17:1-13.

> "And after six days Jesus took Peter, James, and John his brother, and brought them up into a high mountain apart. 2
> And He was transfigured before them. And His face shone as the sun, and His clothing was white as the light. 3 And behold,
> there appeared to them Moses and Elijah talking with Him. 4
> And Peter answered and said to Jesus, Lord, it is good for us to be here. If You will, let us make here three tabernacles;
> one for You, and one for Moses, and one for Elijah. 5 While
> he yet spoke, behold, a bright cloud overshadowed them. And behold a voice out of the cloud which said, This is My
> beloved Son in whom I am well pleased, hear Him. 6 And
> when the disciples heard, they fell on their face and were
> greatly terrified. 7 And Jesus came and touched them, and
> said, Arise and do not be terrified. 8 And lifting up their eyes,
> they saw no one except Jesus alone. 9 And as they came
> down from the mountain, Jesus commanded them, saying, Tell the vision to no one until the Son of man has risen from
> the dead. 10 And His disciples asked Him, saying, Why
> then do the scribes say that Elijah must come first? 11 And
> answering Jesus said to them, Elijah truly shall come first and
> restore all things. 12 But I say to you that Elijah has come
> already, and they did not know him, but have done to him whatever they desired. Likewise also the Son of man shall
> suffer from them. 13 Then His disciples understood that He
> spoke to them about John the Baptist."

Jesus declared: Elijah is coming first and will restore all things and Elijah has already come,—how could that be possible? I believe that He was speaking about John the Baptist, but He was also speaking about "an Elijah company" (a group of Believers moving in the spirit and power of Elijah, like John the Baptist did) in the earth before the final return of Jesus. To further add to this notion, we must also look at John's statements concerning himself—John 1:19-28.

> "And this is the witness of John, when the Jews sent priests and Levites from Jerusalem to ask him, Who are you? 20 And he confessed and did not deny, but confessed, I am not the Christ. 21: And they asked him, What then? Are you Elijah? And he says, I am not. Are you that prophet? And he answered, No. 22 Then they said to him, Who are you so that we may give an answer to those who sent us? What do you say of yourself? 23 He said, I *am* "the voice of one crying in the wilderness: Make straight the way of the Lord," as the prophet Isaiah said. 24 And they who were sent were from the Pharisees. 25 And they asked him and said, Why then do you baptize, if you are not the Christ, nor Elijah, nor that Prophet? 26 John answered them, saying, I baptize with water, but One stands among you whom you do not know. 27 He it is who, coming after me, who has been before me; of whom I am not worthy to loosen the thong of His sandal. 28: These things were done in Bethabara beyond Jordan, where John was baptizing."

Here we note the accurate testimony of John concerning himself as he made some very pertinent statements and declared—that *he was not Elijah*! However, let us extract eight specifics about John's life as it relates to what the Lord is doing in this hour: We will explore Luke 7:24-27; Luke 1:13-17.

- In Luke 7:24-27, Jesus declared that John was "more (not better) than" a Prophet:
  - I submit to you that Jesus was speaking about an apostolic dimension operating in John's life. The Church of Jesus Christ is built upon the foundation of the Apostles and Prophets with Jesus Christ being the Chief Cornerstone. The apostolic and prophetic was and still is an inseparable ministry in the Church of Jesus Christ.
- The Angel spoke to his father Zacharias and specifically told him

that his son was to be called John:

- This instruction from God was awesome when we understand the significance as to what took place. It was the Jewish custom for the son of the High Priest to be named after his father—Luke 1:59. However, the Lord wanted them to break with religious tradition and customs to establish the Forerunner to Jesus. In like manner the Lord is causing His Five-Fold ministers who would sound His trumpet in this hour to break with tradition and religiosity to proclaim the way of the Lord and to make ready a people!

- His father was silenced by the Holy Spirit:
    - Oh, I tell you many religious orders are being shut in this season. They do not have the revelation of what the Lord is doing in the earth even though many of them were used to birth the "spiritual John's" of this hour—Luke 1:19-22.
- Many will rejoice at his birth:
    - John's birth caused many to rejoice because he signalled a new mentality to Kingdom activity, which was Kingdom violence. He was able to bring forth the *manifestation* of the words prophesied by the law and the Prophets. He also brought joy to many because he declared the Messiah to them.
- He did not drink wine nor strong drink:
    - Wine is a mocker of the true anointing and strong drink causes us to forget the law—, which is *self-government*! John was truly a man of internal self-government and that caused him to be intensely focused. This is a reflection of the Nazirite vow, which was accompanied by the fact that no razor was to come upon the head. Hair represents authority, and hair being cut was a sign of one's authority being severed. Ergo, this apostolic-prophetic anointing that is being released today will move into a stronger place of self-government and authority in the things of the Spirit.
- Filled with the Spirit of the Lord:
    - This is powerful, as it is a higher dimension than that of earthly fathering or mentoring. This is the realm of divine impartation, fathering and release. John's father, Zacharias, could not

father or mentor or release him into the accurate spiritual dimension of what God had ordained for him to accomplish. Zacharias was in unbelief and functioned under an old order, which was about to change with the ministry of his son John. Therefore God Himself had to mentor and train John. God's input gave John the power and anointing to function the way he did and released him to be able to identify the Christ—Our Saviour and Lord! There is a dimension of the revelation of Christ that the Lord is bringing forth through the apostolic-prophetic that is designed to turn many to the Lord. There is going to be a new release in the evangelistic realm because of the release of this apostolic-prophetic anointing.

- The power to turn the hearts of fathers, children and the disobedient:
    - An awesome anointing for impartation and wisdom is released through this apostolic-prophetic anointing. There is also the ability to release true fatherhood from a position of strength and purity. The spirit of impartation and wisdom is also very active in this anointing.
- To make a people prepared for the Lord:
    - There is a finishing anointing that is also released through this apostolic\prophetic anointing that is being released in this hour. The final product will be a people who are absolutely ready for the final return of the Lord.

You may have observed that this is the reason that Apostles and Prophets do not have popular ministries because our voices irritate! Our voices are trumpets dealing with sin, pride, religion, etc. Our Message is very clear; therefore we all need to clean up our act so that we could enter the Greatest Feast—The Feast of Tabernacles!

Now, let us re-visit the life of Elijah to better understand our role preceding the return of Jesus. In 1 Kings 17 and 18, we have an account and as we read through the life of this great man of God we should note that everything that happened in his life was training for him, for his great Mt. Carmel experience.

- God raised him up to change an apostate nation by clashing with powers of darkness over the nation.

- He confronted, as one man, 450 false prophets of Baal upon Mt. Carmel.
- This is the one single event that changed the nation and turned Israel back to God, and also revealed the power and glory of God to the people.

Exploring The Pillars Of Elijah's Life

He Addresses A Patriarchal God!

1 Kings 18:36—"Lord God of Abraham, Isaac and Israel..." He knows that God is a God that has worked throughout the generations and can now work in his generation. He goes on "*let it be known this day!" Not in somebody else's day! But today in our day!*

He Was A Man Of Pure Commitment

1 Kings 18:21—"And Elijah came to all the people, and said, "How long will you falter between two opinions? If the LORD *is* God, follow Him; but if Baal, follow him." But the people answered him not a word." Elijah's pure commitment to God is reflected here, as the very first thing he does is to call the people to make a choice between Baal and God. The spirit and power of Elijah goes against complacency and worldliness. It confronts the religious spirit that makes people become hearers of the Word but not doers. It attacks the very demonic power that causes the "Word of God to be ineffective"—Mark 7:5-13. It also attacks the spirit that causes one to have a "form of godliness, but denying the power thereof"—2 Timothy 3:5. It draws a line between the holy and the profane and pushes people to a place of "*Pure Commitment*".

He Was A True Leader

1 Kings 18:30—"Then Elijah said to all the people, "Come near to me." So all the people came near to him.

And he repaired the altar of the LORD *that was* broken down." What a tender statement! This is the heart of a true leader, he does not send people away in their confusion, but seeks to draw them near. The true Elijah anointing while it is aggressive and confrontational on the outside, is very gentile and people-oriented on the inside. It wants to confront people with the view of bringing them closer to God. Apostles

Peter and John bring out this dimension very clearly in their account in Acts 3:1-10, which I will look at in greater, detail later on.

Let Us Repair The Altar

1 Kings 18:31-32—"And Elijah took twelve stones, according to the number of the tribes of the sons of Jacob, to whom the word of the LORD had come, saying, "Israel shall be your name." 32 Then with the stones he built an altar in the name of the LORD; and he made a trench around the altar large enough to hold two seahs of seed." Altars represent places of sacrifice and true commitment! The Elijah spirit always seeks to push people to return to the Altar—Romans 12:1.

Elijah restores the Altar and then goes on to prepare the sacrifice. Restoration is another characteristic of the Elijah anointing! It is also an aspect to what we as apostolic people are called to do. We want to see pure worship restored, pure communion restored, commitment restored, we want to see man restored to the Almighty God!

Drawing Near To God

1 Kings 18:36-39—"And it came to pass, at the time of the offering of the evening sacrifice, that Elijah the prophet came near and said, "Lord God of Abraham, Isaac, and Israel, let it be known this day that You are God in Israel and I am Your servant, and that I have done all these things at Your word. 37 Hear me, O Lord, hear me, that this people may know that You are the Lord God, and that You have turned their hearts back to You again." 38 Then the fire of the Lord fell and consumed the burnt sacrifice, and the wood and the stones and the dust, and it licked up the water that was in the trench. 39 Now when all the people saw it, they fell on their faces; and they said, "The Lord, He is God! The Lord, He is God!"

Verse 36 gives us the key to unlock the door to the Power of God! At the time of the evening sacrifice Elijah *draws near to God!* This is awesome, for as we draw near to God we cannot help but be pure and holy and by doing this, it releases the Lord to do great and mighty things through us. For the Word of God says that as we "draw near to God, He will draw near to us" and when this happens cleansing and purification take place, resulting in the Lord bringing elevation to us—James 4:8-10. We are not called to pray empty prayers that cannot breakthrough! We are called to pray with strength, wisdom and intensity.

His Major Enemy Was Jezebel

Here are some dynamics of this Jezebel spirit: The name Jezebel means—"un-cohabited". The woman sporting this name was very much married. So in essence Jezebel means "one who is uncovered or one that will not submit to authority". Although we are considering this woman's name and what it means, please understand that this is not a woman thing; *it is a spirit that affects both male and female*. It is an unclean spirit that seeks to manipulate and control governmental authority, and can only function effectively whenever there is weak leadership as exemplified in her husband Ahab.

> "But there was no one like Ahab who sold himself to do wickedness in the sight of the LORD, *because Jezebel his wife stirred him up*. 26 And he behaved very abominably in following idols, according to all that the Amorites had done, whom the LORD had cast out before the children of Israel." [Italics added] 1 Kings 21:25-26

Jezebel was not simply an Old Testament travesty but a power to be reckoned with even today as the *Lord warned us of this spirit* entering into the New Testament Church. Jezebel disguises itself in the prophetic realm where it rises up in an attempt to bring revelation to the Church by means of teaching. But in direct opposition to the true Elijah anointing and spirit of the true prophetic, this false prophetess brings a [10]counterfeit of the true apostolic ministry being restored in the Church today. She uses seduction as her main tactic. Seduction is a cunning, well-planned, system of attack with the sole intent of misleading and deceiving.

> "Nevertheless I have a few things against you, because you allow *that woman Jezebel, who calls herself a prophetess, to teach and seduce* My servants to commit sexual immorality and eat things sacrificed to idols." [Italics added] Revelation 2:20

---

10 2 Corinthians 11:13-15

The spirit of Jezebel can manifest through highly capable and gifted persons who through legitimate alliance, hold keys to policy and influence over decisions. This spirit loves to work from within leadership, to deflect worship from God to a "leader," "owner," "master," "husband," or "father" whose permissiveness will allow for idolatry and sexual looseness that accelerates with time. In essence this spirit seeks "weak, compromising leaders" and begin to work with them to corrupt the church or Saints.

God, by His Spirit, has already released the prophetic and apostolic anointing to destroy the spirit of Jezebel—a false prophetic-apostolic spirit—in His Church. In the Book of Revelation, He declared:

> "And to the angel of the church in Thyatira write, 'These things says the Son of God, who has eyes like a flame of fire, and His feet like fine brass: 19 "I know your works, love, service, faith, and your patience; and as for your works, the last are more than the first. 20 Nevertheless I have a few things against you, because *you allow that woman Jezebel, who calls herself a Prophetess*, [*false prophetic ministry*] to *teach* [*a type of false apostolic ministry*] and *seduce My servants* to commit sexual immorality and eat things sacrificed to idols. 21 And I gave her time to repent of her sexual immorality, and she did not repent. 22 Indeed I will cast her into a sickbed, and those who commit adultery with her into great tribulation, unless they repent of their deeds. 23 *I will kill her children with death*, and all the churches shall know that I am He who searches the minds and hearts. And I will give to each one of you according to your works." [Italics and parenthesis added] Revelation 2:18-23

Points To Note:

- The spirit of Jezebel will be active in the New Testament Church.
- It will manifest itself in the prophetic and apostolic realms.
- It will carry a strong seductive emphasis.
- It will be empowered to attempt to cause the servants of God to commit sexual immorality.
- It will also have a strong spirit of deception.

In order to defeat this Jezebel spirit that is masquerading in the Church the Lord is using Apostles and Prophets.

However, just are there are true Apostles and Prophets, there are false ones as well; hence the reason there is such a strong emphasis to try those who claim to be Apostles! Please understand that not everyone carrying the title of "Apostle" is sent by God.

> "To the angel of the church of Ephesus write, 'These things says He who holds the seven stars in His right hand, who walks in the midst of the seven golden lampstands: 2 "I know your works, your labour, your patience, and that you cannot bear those who are evil. And *you have tested those who say they are Apostles and are not, and have found them liars*." [Italics added] Revelation 2:1-2

While the scope of this writing is not to define that which constitutes being an Apostle, I would like to briefly re-visit the Apostle Paul's warning to us about these false apostles and false ministers rising up in the Church.

> "For I consider that I am not at all inferior to the most eminent Apostles. 6 Even though I am untrained in speech, yet I am not in knowledge. But we have been thoroughly manifested among you in all things. 7 Did I commit sin in humbling myself that you might be exalted, because I preached the gospel of God to you free of charge? "...13 But what I do, I will also continue to do, that I may cut off the opportunity from those who desire an opportunity to be regarded just as we are in the things of which they boast. 14 *For such are false Apostles, deceitful workers, transforming themselves into Apostles of Christ*. And no wonder! For satan himself transforms himself into an angel of light. 15 Therefore it is no great thing if his ministers also transform themselves into ministers of righteousness, whose end will be according to their works." [Italics added] 2 Corinthians 11:5-7, 12-15

Remember The Wise Words Of Apostle Paul:

> "For the weapons of our warfare are not carnal but mighty in God for pulling down strongholds, 5 casting down arguments and every high thing that exalts itself against the knowledge of God, bringing every thought into captivity to the obedience of Christ, and being ready to punish all disobedience when your obedience is fulfilled." 2 Corinthians 10:4-6

While not everyone who carries the title "Apostle" is an Apostle; we need to understand that this does not make them a false minister or a false Christian. Some people will be misguided or misdirected in simply seeking a title, and we need to discern accurately in order to rightly restore the person. As with every move of God, there is emphasis placed on what the Holy Spirit is seeking to accomplish. In this case it is the restoration of Apostles, which has become a "*buzz word*" in the Church. Because of this, many are being called Apostle and some rightly so, while others are being called "Apostle" erroneously. This is why we will need wisdom and the true [11]"*fathering anointing*" to discern and implement the right course of action in dealing with the ones who say they are Apostles and are not.

Again let me re-emphasize that it will take apostolic wisdom and warfare strength along with prophetic vision and tenacity to defeat and destroy the spirit of Jezebel in these days. And make no mistake about this: the Jezebel spirit is alive and active in the Church today! This is why there must be a return to the biblical pattern of Church Leadership and Governmental Structure, which is recorded in the Word.

> "And God has *appointed* [*set*] these in the church: first Apostles, second Prophets, third Teachers, after that miracles, then gifts of healings, helps, administration, varieties of tongues." [Italics and parenthesis added] 1 Corinthians 12:28

The word "*set*" or "*appoint*" is from the Greek word "kathistemi", which is translated—"to appoint to a permanent position or office." In this sense the verb is often translated "to make" or "to set," in

11 You can read the author's book "Five Pillars of The Apostolic" for a more in-depth analysis on the "fathering anointing". See ordering details at the end of this book.

appointing a person to a place of authority. So the verse could read as follows:

> "And God has [permanently] *appointed* these [positions or offices] in the church: first Apostles, second Prophets, third Teachers, after that miracles, then gifts of healings, helps, administrations, varieties of tongues." [Parenthesis added]

It is vital that we recognize this order so that we can maintain healthy churches. It is indeed sad when so many churches do not and will not recognize this order set out by the Lord. Because of this, we have allowed the spirit of Jezebel to enter the ranks of the Body of Christ. However, we thank the Lord that great light is now being shed on these issues and change is being seen at an accelerated speed. Many churches are now accepting the fact that [12]Apostles are for today and did not cease to exist when the early Apostles died!

The spirit of Jezebel will only be vanquished with a strong Governmental Church operating on the earth, where true Apostles and Prophets are given their rightful place to function. [13]This is the only way to defeat this Jezebel spirit.

The blowing of trumpets was also significance for the journeying of the Camps—Numbers 10:3-6 "When they blow both of them, all the congregation shall gather before you at the door of the tabernacle of meeting. 4 But if they blow *only* one, then the leaders, the heads of the divisions of Israel, shall gather to you. 5 When you sound the advance, the camps that lie on the east side shall then begin their journey. 6 When you sound the advance the second time, then the camps that lie on the south side shall begin their journey; they shall sound the call for them to begin their journeys."

The Church has camped long enough and it is time to go forward and take the Promised Land. It is okay to camp, however, when the Trumpet sounds you have to be ready to pick up your tents and move on. There is a Trumpet call in this hour for the Church to move forward. *Only those who have the ears to hear will hear what the Spirit is saying*!

---

12 You can read the author's trilogy of books on The Apostolic. See ordering details at the end of this book.

13 For more on this you can read the author's book "Identifying and Defeating the Jezebel Spirit". See ordering details at the end of this book.

The blowing of trumpets was also significance in preparing of the people for war—Numbers 10:9 "When you go to war in your land against the enemy who oppresses you, then you shall sound an alarm with the trumpets, and you will be remembered before the Lord your God, and you will be saved from your enemies." There is indeed an aggressive, militant Church rising in the earth, declaring war on the devil's war!—Oh Army of God *arise* and take up your Sword!

The blowing of Trumpets was also used in announcing the celebration of the Feasts—Numbers 10:10 "Also in the day of your gladness, in your appointed feasts, and at the beginning of your months, you shall blow the trumpets over your burnt offerings and over the sacrifices of your peace offerings; and they shall be a memorial for you before your God: I am the Lord your God."

The Day of Atonement

The Day of Atonement was a very significant day as it was the holiest day of the year for the Israelites. This was the day that prayer and fasting was done and sacrifices were made for sin. It represented the cleansing of their lives in preparation for the Year of Jubilee. The details for this Feast are found in Leviticus 16:6-34.

> "Aaron shall offer the bull as a sin offering, which is for himself, and make atonement for himself and for his house. 7 He shall take the two goats and present them before the LORD at the door of the tabernacle of meeting. 8 Then Aaron shall cast lots for the two goats: one lot for the LORD and the other lot for the scapegoat. 9 And Aaron shall bring the goat on which the LORD's lot fell, and offer it as a sin offering. 10 But the goat on which the lot fell to be the scapegoat shall be presented alive before the LORD, to make atonement upon it, and to let it go as the scapegoat into the wilderness. 11 "And Aaron shall bring the bull of the sin offering, which is for himself, and make atonement for himself and for his house, and shall kill the bull as the sin offering which is for himself. 12 Then he shall take a censer full of burning coals of fire from the altar before the LORD, with his hands full of sweet incense beaten fine, and

bring it inside the veil. 13 And he shall put the incense on the fire before the LORD, that the cloud of incense may cover the mercy seat that is on the Testimony, lest he die. 14 He shall take some of the blood of the bull and sprinkle it with his finger on the mercy seat on the east side; and before the mercy seat he shall sprinkle some of the blood with his finger seven times. 15 "Then he shall kill the goat of the sin offering, which is for the people, bring its blood inside the veil, do with that blood as he did with the blood of the bull, and sprinkle it on the mercy seat and before the mercy seat. 16 So he shall make atonement for the Holy Place, because of the uncleanness of the children of Israel, and because of their transgressions, for all their sins; and so he shall do for the tabernacle of meeting which remains among them in the midst of their uncleanness. 17 There shall be no man in the tabernacle of meeting when he goes in to make atonement in the Holy Place, until he comes out, that he may make atonement for himself, for his household, and for all the assembly of Israel. 18 And he shall go out to the altar that is before the LORD, and make atonement for it, and shall take some of the blood of the bull and some of the blood of the goat, and put it on the horns of the altar all around. 19 Then he shall sprinkle some of the blood on it with his finger seven times, cleanse it, and consecrate it from the uncleanness of the children of Israel. 20 "And when he has made an end of atoning for the Holy Place, the tabernacle of meeting, and the altar, he shall bring the live goat. 21 Aaron shall lay both his hands on the head of the live goat, confess over it all the iniquities of the children of Israel, and all their transgressions, concerning all their sins, putting them on the head of the goat, and shall send it away into the wilderness by the hand of a suitable man. 22 The goat shall bear on itself all their iniquities to an uninhabited land; and he shall release the goat in the wilderness. 23 "Then Aaron shall come into the tabernacle of meeting, shall take off the linen garments which he put on when he went into the Holy Place, and shall leave them there. 24 And he shall wash his body with water in a holy place, put on his garments, come out and offer his burnt offering and the burnt offering of the people, and make atonement for himself and for the people. 25 The fat of the sin offering he shall burn on the altar. 26 And he who released the goat as the scapegoat shall wash his clothes and bathe his body in water, and afterward he may come into the camp. 27 The bull for the sin offering and the goat for the sin offering, whose blood was brought in to make atonement in the Holy Place, shall be carried outside the camp. And they shall burn in the fire their skins, their flesh, and their offal. 28 Then he who burns them shall wash his clothes and bathe his body in water, and afterward he may come into the camp. 29 "This shall be a statute forever for you: In the seventh month, on the tenth day of the month, you shall afflict your souls, and do no work at all, whether a native of your own country or a stranger who dwells among you. 30 For on that day the priest shall make atonement for you, to cleanse you, that you may be clean from all your sins before the LORD. 31 It is a sabbath of solemn rest for you, and you shall afflict your souls. It is a statute forever. 32 And the priest, who is anointed and consecrated to minister as priest in his father's place, shall make atonement, and put on the linen clothes, the holy garments; 33 then he shall make atonement for the Holy Sanctuary, and he shall make atonement for the tabernacle of meeting and for the altar, and he shall make atonement for the priests and for all the people of the assembly. 34 This shall be an everlasting statute for you, to make atonement for the children of Israel, for all their sins, once a year." And he did as the LORD commanded Moses."

"Also the tenth day of this seventh month shall be the Day of Atonement. It shall be a holy convocation for you; you shall afflict your souls, and offer an offering made by fire to the LORD. 28 And you shall do no work on that same day, for it is the Day of Atonement, to make atonement for you before the LORD your God. 29 For any person who is not afflicted in soul on that same day shall be cut off from his people. 30 And any person who does any work on that same day, that person I will destroy from among his people. 31 You shall do no manner of work; it shall be a statute forever throughout your generations in all your dwellings. 32 It shall be to you a sabbath of solemn rest, and you shall afflict your souls; on the ninth day of the month at evening, from evening to evening, you shall celebrate your sabbath." Leviticus 23:27-32

Several things about this Day:

1. It was a Holy Convocation—Convocation was the official calling of a sacred assembly to worship the Lord, and it was marked by the fact that *no work* was to be done!
2. On day ten of the seventh month, God chose as a day of cleansing—Leviticus 23:27.
   The number ten in Biblical terms denotes the number for judgement and atonement! Ten = Trial, Testing and Judgement:
   - For example the Ten Commandments—Exodus 20:1-17.
   - Daniel and friends while in Babylon asked that they be tested for ten days—Daniel 1:12.
   - In the Book of Revelation we are told: "Do not fear any of those things which you are about to suffer. Indeed, the devil is about to throw some of you into prison, that you may be tested, and you will have tribulation ten days. Be faithful until death, and I will give you the crown of life."—Revelation 2:10.
3. There will be *experiential deliverance* from sin for God's people as seen in Leviticus 16:19-21—it will do us well to remember these words spoken by the Lord in the following—Matthew 5:48; John 17:21-23 Romans 6:4-11; Romans 8:2; Galatians 5:24; 1 John 3:3, 6-9!
4. On the Day of Atonement Aaron the High Priest entered *beyond The Veil*. Oh this is so awesome, as we remember that Jesus, our "Aaron," our "High Priest" has not only entered beyond the veil, He tore the veil from top to bottom over 2000 years ago, giving us the liberty to enter the Throne room of God. So now is time for us to experientially walk in the fullness of entering into His Presence—Hebrews 6:20 and Hebrews 10:19-25! We will also see in this season the true unveiling of the "Sons of God" (this is not gender specific)—Romans 8:19; John 7:14 It was at the Feast of Tabernacles that Jesus began to "unveil" Himself—John 7:1-18; Revelation 12:1-5!

The next thing that happens on the Day of Atonement is the blowing of the Jubilee Trumpet recorded in Leviticus 25:9 "Then you shall cause the trumpet of the Jubilee to sound on the tenth *day* of the seventh month; on the Day of Atonement you shall make the trumpet to sound throughout all your land."

The Year Of Jubilee

The concept of the Jubilee was a special year of remission of sins and universal pardon. In the Book of Leviticus, a Jubilee year is mentioned to occur every fiftieth year, in which slaves and prisoners would be freed, debts would be forgiven and the mercies of God would be particularly manifest—Leviticus 25:1-55; 27:17-24. Especially Leviticus 25:8-17.

> "'And you shall count seven sabbaths of years for yourself, seven times seven years; and the time of the seven sabbaths of years shall be to you forty-nine years. 9 Then you shall cause the trumpet of the Jubilee to sound on the tenth *day* of the seventh month; on the Day of Atonement you shall make the trumpet to sound throughout all your land. 10 And you shall consecrate the fiftieth year, and proclaim liberty throughout *all* the land to all its inhabitants. It shall be a Jubilee for you; and each of you shall return to his possession, and each of you shall return to his family. 11 That fiftieth year shall be a Jubilee to you; in it you shall neither sow nor reap what grows of its own accord, nor gather *the grapes* of your untended vine. 12 For it *is* the Jubilee; it shall be holy to you; you shall eat its produce from the field. 13 'In this Year of Jubilee, each of you shall return to his possession. 14 And if you sell anything to your neighbour or buy from your neighbour's hand, you shall not oppress one another. 15 According to the number of years after the Jubilee you shall buy from your neighbour, and according to the number of years of crops he shall sell to you. 16 According to the multitude of years you shall increase its price, and according to the fewer number of years you shall diminish its price; for he sells to you *according* to the number

> *of the years* of the crops. 17 Therefore you shall not oppress one another, but you shall fear your God; for I *am* the LORD your God."

1. This was known as the "acceptable year"—Isaiah 61:2 and also as the "year of liberty"—Ezekiel 46:17
2. Every 50th year three things were to be accomplished:
    - All debts were forgiven.
    - All slaves were released.
    - All land reverted to its original owner.

As Believers in Jesus Christ we keep the feast by faith and not in the natural realm, as the Israelites were commanded to do before Jesus Christ came and offered His Life as the Perfect Sacrifice. We are talking here about spiritual dimensions. In Exodus 34:23-24 there is a powerful promise given by the Lord every time the feasts are kept:

- Casting out devils before us—Full deliverance from demonic spirits.
- Enlarging of our borders—Going beyond our natural abilities. I want that!
- Breaking of the spirit of covetousness and theft!—Loving our brothers as ourselves.

Things that were hindering and blocking us will be removed and enlargement will come. The Spirit of God moves mightily when we call people to the Mountains—when we call/encourage the Saints to go up higher, in their spiritual lives, for example Isaiah 25:6-12.

> "And on this Mount [Zion] shall the Lord of hosts make for all peoples a feast of rich things [symbolic of His coronation festival inaugurating the reign of the Lord on earth, in the wake of a background of gloom, judgment, and terror], a feast of wines on the lees—of fat things full of marrow, of wines on the lees well refined. 7 And He will destroy on this mountain the covering of the face that is cast over the heads of all peoples [in mourning], and the veil [of profound wretchedness] that is woven and spread over all nations. 8 He will swallow up death

> [in victory; He will abolish death forever]. And the Lord God will wipe away tears from all faces; and the reproach of His people He will take away from off all the earth; for the Lord has spoken it. 9 It shall be said in that day, Behold our God upon Whom we have waited and hoped, that He might save us! This is the Lord, we have waited for Him; we will be glad and rejoice in His salvation. 10 For the hand of the Lord shall rest on this Mount [Zion], and Moab shall be threshed and trodden down in his place as straw is trodden down in the [filthy] water of a [primitive] cesspit. 11 And though [Moab] stretches forth his hands in the midst of [the filthy water] as a swimmer stretches out his hands to swim, the Lord will bring down [Moab's] pride in spite of the skilfulness of his hands and together with the spoils of his hands. 12 And the high fortifications of your walls [the Lord] will bring down, lay low, and bring to the ground, even to the dust."

1. There will be a feast of rich things or choice pieces.
2. A feast of fat things of marrow.
3. A feast of well-refined wines on the lees.
4. Revelation will come—the veil that is cast over the people will be broken.
5. The veil over the nations will be lifted and destroyed.
6. Death will be swallowed up forever.
7. Tears will be wiped away.
8. He will take away our rebuke from the earth.

AWESOME! Totally AWESOME!!!

As we close this chapter let me say this: This is what the Feast of Tabernacles is bringing to the Church! Unity! The Book of Ephesians speaks clearly about it and Jesus also prayed that it would happen in John Chapter 17!

> "I, therefore, the prisoner of the Lord, beseech you to walk worthy of the calling with which you were called, 2 with all lowliness and gentleness, with longsuffering, bearing with one another in love, 3 endeavouring to keep the unity of the Spirit

in the bond of peace. 4 There is one body and one Spirit, just as you were called in one hope of your calling; 5 one Lord, one faith, one baptism; 6 one God and Father of all, who is above all, and through all, and in you all... 11 And He Himself gave some to be apostles, some prophets, some evangelists, and some pastors and teachers, 12 for the equipping of the saints for the work of ministry, for the edifying of the body of Christ, 13 till we all come to the unity of the faith and of the knowledge of the Son of God, to a perfect man, to the measure of the stature of the fullness of Christ..." [Italics added] Ephesians 4:1-6, 11-13

"I pray for them. I do not pray for the world but for those whom You have given Me, for they are Yours. 10 And all Mine are Yours, and Yours are Mine, and I am glorified in them. 11 Now I am no longer in the world, but these are in the world, and I come to You. Holy Father, keep through Your name those whom You have given Me, that they may be one as We are... 20 "I do not pray for these alone, but also for those who will believe in Me through their word; 21 that they all may be one, as You, Father, are in Me, and I in You; that they also may be one in Us, that the world may believe that You sent Me. 22 And the glory which You gave Me I have given them, that they may be one just as We are one: 23 I in them, and You in Me; that they may be made perfect in one, and that the world may know that You have sent Me, and have loved them as You have loved Me." [Italics added] John 17:9-11, 20-23

Are we there yet as The Church? Not quite, but we will get there! We know that strong apostolic churches are being raised up for God all over the earth. These churches like Esther are being raised up for a time like this. A time where we are seeing the moral fabric of the Church being attacked and threatened, BUT God will have His way, because like Esther many are already declaring "if we perish we perish, but we are going to work for The King, and see His Church remain Glorious in the nations of the earth".

Chapter Four

Esther: An Apostolic Church

From the onset of this chapter I would like reiterate that we are looking at Esther, whose name meant among many other things, "Myrtle" which is derived from her Hebrew name Hadassah. In classic mythology the myrtle shrub was a symbol of heroism and immortality. For the Hebrews, it typified peace and thanksgiving, and a picture of God's promised blessings! The Myrtle wood was also used to make booths for the Feast of Tabernacles, the final of three very important Feasts, under the Old Covenant.

I believe that Esther in typology also represents the Church that is apostolic in nature (since as Jesus Christ, Who is the Builder of the Church, is the Apostle and what He builds is apostolic). This apostolic dimension is brought out in her function and mandate. Her apostolic function was reflected in her preparation to ascend the throne as she spent 12 months preparing herself to meet King Ahasuerus. In Scripture "12" is the number that represents Government and the apostolic (twelve Apostles)...

Esther's rise to the throne came about because of King Ahasuerus' was dissatisfied with his wife queen Vashti, who refused to submit to his request to appear at a royal banquet—Esther 1:10-22; The king was dismayed by this behaviour and as such he was looking to replace her. Esther was chosen and she became Queen. After some time, a plot to kill her husband King Ahasuerus was revealed to her by her uncle Mordecai. Queen Esther revealed it to King Ahasuerus and when confirmed, he had the perpetrators killed and they hung by their necks in the gallows until dead. Their replacement was Haman, a man who had a deep hatred for the Jews.

Haman's relentless hatred of the Jews influenced the king to issue a decree that all Jews living in the 27 provinces would be put to death within 11 months, Esther 3:8-15.

> "Then Haman said to King Ahasuerus, "There is a certain people scattered and dispersed among the people in all the provinces of your kingdom; their laws are different from all other people's, and they do not keep the king's laws. Therefore it is not fitting for the king to let them remain. 9 If it pleases the king, let a decree be written that they be destroyed, and I will pay ten thousand talents of silver into the hands of those who do the work, to bring it into the king's treasuries." 10 So the king took his signet ring from his hand and gave it to Haman, the son of Hammedatha the Agagite, the enemy of the Jews. 11 And the king said to Haman, "The money and the people are given to you, to do with them as seems good to you." 12 Then the king's scribes were called on the thirteenth day of the first month, and a decree was written according to all that Haman commanded—to the king's satraps, to the governors who were over each province, to the officials of all people, to every province according to its script, and to every people in their language. In the name of King Ahasuerus it was written, and sealed with the king's signet ring. 13 And the letters were sent by couriers into all the king's provinces, to destroy, to kill, and to annihilate all the Jews, both young and old, little children and women, in one day, on the thirteenth day of the twelfth month, which is the month of Adar, and to plunder their possessions. 14 A copy of the document was to be issued as law in every province, being published for all people, that they should be ready for that day. 15 The

> couriers went out, hastened by the king's command; and the decree was proclaimed in Shushan the citadel. So the king and Haman sat down to drink, but the city of Shushan was perplexed."

As was their custom when mourning was upon them, all the Jews were in sackcloth, weeping and wailing. Mordecai gave Esther a challenge before he died. He told her that if she kept quiet before the king she will not escape the death edict either, Esther 4:14—"For if you remain completely silent at this time, relief and deliverance will arise for the Jews from another place, but you and your father's house will perish. Yet who knows whether you have come to the kingdom for such a time as this?"

Deliverance then will arise from another place Mordecai told her. It was here that Ester rose to her call. This is just awesome. Esther is truly the picture of an apostolic people! Esther, like the Church being a woman of incredible courage and destiny rose to the occasion. It is in this framework that we see five attitudes for the Church in this present time, as we too face many challenges from the systems of this world and demonic inspired thrones.

1ST Attitude: The Church Will Come To A New Sense Of Corporate Destiny.

We too have come into the Kingdom for "such a time as this", Esther 4:14. We have come to a royal position for purposes beyond our own personal desires and petty wishes. Crisis often defines destiny. Our present focus is blurred and the pressure of a crisis will cure that. What is our crisis you may ask? It is an identity crisis. Knowing who we are and knowing what our purpose is in life is fulfilling our destiny. The Church of Jesus Christ needs to recapture the full understanding of the fact: "As He is so are we in the world"—1 John 4:17. We must put on our royal robes just as Esther—Esther 5:1. This is not the time to be unsure of who we are. This is not the time to blur the lines between what is right and wrong.

2ND Attitude: A New Level Of Corporate Unity Is Required.

We must all "gather together" just as the Jews in Shushan, who fasted and prayed for three days, Esther 4:16. There are far too many who go it alone, who refuse to be part of a corporate body for whatever reason. We also see at times the wrong people setting the agenda for the Church. With the restoration of true Apostles we will need to come to grips with the fact that as God's generals they are given the responsibility of leading the Church. Through them, the type of unity described in Ephesians 4:3-6 will be maintained. I emphasize maintained and not attained. We cannot attain to something that is given in the Spirit. We walk in it by faith.

3RD Attitude: A New Attitude Of Determination, Patience And Endurance Will Be Instilled In The Church.

One of the primary marks of an Apostle is the enduring character that says, "I don't quit". However, endurance is not just a sign of an Apostle only but also a sign of the Apostolic Church—2 Corinthians 12:12. We too like Esther must say, "If I perish, I perish"—Esther 4:16. Living in a society of ease, comfort and immediate gratification has made us weak in patience and endurance. We have bailed out too soon, failed to cross many finish lines and given up just short of the manifestation of a prayer. Endurance may be the most significant sign of an Apostle, because an Apostle without endurance cannot really be called an Apostle.

The Scripture is very clear when it comes to testing and trying those who claim to be Apostles, and as we shall see endurance is right at the apex of the list of those things to look for in genuine Apostles.

Genuine Ministers—Their Foundation

[14]There has been a significant amount of discussion on judging ministries for oneself. How do we know who is truly called of God, what about false apostles and false prophets? I have taken some time to consider and meditate upon this subject. I feel led to share my

14 An article by Apostle, Lloyd C. Phillips of The Fellow Laborer's International Network.

thoughts with you which include some practical application in light of the ministry of apostleship, and how to discern true, false, functioning, fallen, or those simply immature in ministry. These are my thoughts, based upon study of the Scripture, which to the best of my ability has been "rightly divided" in light of my scope and understanding of Scripture.

In 2 Corinthians 12:12 (KJV) the Apostle Paul wrote what he called the signs of an Apostle. "Truly the signs of an Apostle were wrought among you in all patience, in signs, and wonders, and mighty deeds." Paul is clearly speaking of his apostleship in this verse, and in the immediate context of this verse. He was not defending his Christianity as no one questioned that he was a Christian, not even Emperor Nero. However, men came into Corinth and caused the church there to question his ministry, which he was defending. In my own characterization of Apostles and the Apostolic Movement I have never made excuses to those who want to see more signs and wonders. I'd like to see more of them myself—when will we ever have experienced enough of God's miracle working power? However, we should be reminded that the Pharisees demanded more signs and wonders from Jesus Christ Himself. So we might draw some understanding from this worldly judgement. Specifically, that if some people could not even be satisfied with the miracles and signs which Jesus Christ did, why would you try to impress them? God doesn't.

When Jesus Christ left His commission with His Apostles and Disciples He said in Mark 16:17-18, "And these signs shall follow them that believe; In my name shall they cast out devils; they shall speak with new tongues; They shall take up serpents; and if they drink any deadly thing, it shall not hurt them; they shall lay hands on the sick, and they shall recover." The only requirement the Lord gave for these signs was to believe. Those who would have faith to accomplish these things in His Name (His Authority) would be known as Believers. I often like to jokingly say at this point that I usually prefer for people to become Believers before they become Leaders. Get my point? These signs were simply the signs of Believers. These are not signs of apostleship; these are just the "regular kind of every day signs." The signs Paul was speaking of were of the same general variety, but they were accomplished in the course of his apostolic ministry.

There is one thing which I notice that is often overlooked in 2 Corinthians 12:12. Paul began his list with patience, not with miracles. Now the Greek word hupomone, translated patience in this verse is translated perseverance or endurance in other places. Nevertheless, I point it out here because I believe it is an attribute, which Paul was using to set apart his apostleship from the everyday, garden-variety, apostleship, generally willing to be martyred at a moments notice, First Century Christian attitude.

Once I was speaking with a young man who was going through what you might call a “rebellious stage.” He had decided that he no longer believed in Apostles and Prophets because he wasn’t seeing “enough miracles.” His proof text was 2 Corinthians 12:12. I pointed out Mark 16:17-18, and reminded him that all Saints should manifest supernatural signs and wonders, and that a difference in the two texts was that Paul pointed to his patience. I then reminded the young man, with a loving smile, that those around him were currently exercising great patience with him. He thought for a moment and then agreed and added that he knew he was only saved and alive because of the miracles of God.

In short, I am saying that Paul was pointing to the importance of apostolic character and endurance before signs (but not to replace them). If we look only for supernatural signs first and foremost, I believe we will place ourselves in danger of eventually being deceived, led astray, or in the least be hurt unnecessarily. Am I saying that signs are unimportant? Not at all, simply that we should look for the Character of Jesus Christ first. After all, in the heart of every true Minister is the desire that Christ would be formed in His people. How can a Minister truly assist Jesus Christ being formed in His people if His Character is not first being formed in the Minister? Could the Apostle Paul say: “Imitate me, just as I also imitate Christ,”—1 Corinthians 11:1 if he wasn’t imitating Him closely? Jesus Christ said simply concerning Disciples and Ministers that we could know them by their fruit.

Now for the longest time I was constrained to overlook poor character in Ministers because there was supernatural power and the fruit, which appeared to accompany that power. Over time, and with a lot of hard-won learning, I found that a lot of the fruit that manifested did not remain, and also some of what I thought was fruit was not spiritually nutritious at all. I sought the Lord on this question, seeking a way to discern much more quickly the fruit in a ministry so I would not have to expend so much time, and often experience so much hurt and disappointment. May I share with you what His Spirit said to me? He said simply, "you will know them by their fruit."

Now I had a dilemma. I thought I was right back where I had begun, and then it dawned on me that I'd been looking at the fruit from the *ministry*, rather than the fruit from the *Minister*. There is an important difference. Paul said, "But the fruit of the Spirit is love, joy, peace, longsuffering, [patience] kindness, goodness, faithfulness"—Galatians 5:22. I now realized that I could look for these attributes in the Minister's life and spend a lot less time deciding if I would submit myself to the ministry. Now I spend a lot less time in disappointment from a Minister who "did me wrong," or led me wrong. I simply do not submit myself to a ministry where I do not see *the Character of Jesus Christ more clearly exemplified than any other attributes*. Am I saying that a Minister cannot be from God if they are not exhibiting the fruit of the Spirit? No—not at all.

Once I was speaking to the Lord about a particular Minister who had become somewhat of a "thorn in the flesh" to me in a number of ways. I was surprised when the Lord answered me and said; "I'm surprised at you, you should know that I use arrogant, controlling people all the time." Then He complemented these words with a vision. In the vision two carpenters came to work on a building. One worked in pride, one worked in humility. At the end of the day, the Lord only paid the humble carpenter. Then I realized that the Lord as The Master Builder was showing me that He is going to put anyone to work on His building that can "swing a hammer". But according to His own rule, if anyone does not work according to His plan, that person will have no inheritance—2 Timothy 2:5 And also if anyone competes in athletics, he is not crowned unless he competes according to the rules.—Also 1 Corinthians 3:14,15 13:3; Galatians 5:21 etc...

Apostle Paul placed the majority of the proof of his apostleship upon the apostolic endurance, which he modelled for others to follow. In a number of places the Apostle Paul defined his apostleship and even exposed false apostleship by pointing out the many trials he endured and overcome—often supernaturally—for the sake of the Gospel.

> "Are they ministers of Christ?; I speak as a fool; I am more: in labours more abundant, in stripes above measure, in prisons more frequently, in deaths often. 24 From the Jews five times I received forty stripes minus one. 25 Three times I was beaten with rods; once I was stoned; three times I was shipwrecked; a night and a day I have been in the deep; 26 in journeys often, in perils of waters, in perils of robbers, in perils of my own countrymen, in perils of the Gentiles, in perils in the city, in perils in the wilderness, in perils in the sea, in perils among false brethren; 27 in weariness and toil, in sleeplessness often, in hunger and thirst, in fastings often, in cold and nakedness; 28 besides the other things, what comes upon me daily: my deep concern for all the churches." 1 Corinthians 11:23-28

Paul placed such a high assessment upon apostolic patience and endurance that he made it a pattern for others to follow in their ministry, 1 Timothy 1:16 says: "However, for this reason I obtained mercy, that in me first Jesus Christ might *show all longsuffering, as a pattern* to those who are going to believe on Him for everlasting life." I am not saying that apostolic ministry must be perfect, only perfected. The character of patient endurance must be a foundation for the signs, wonders and miracles, and these manifestations are no replacement for and Minister or Believer's character. We may choose personally to disassociate ourselves from arrogant, self-promoting, controlling people, and other works of the flesh that we see. We love to associate with the humble, and to be with those who promote Jesus Christ, and boast in the Lord, and glory in their own weaknesses. When the Apostles were brought before the rulers in Acts 4, it was because of a notable miracle. But the miracle did not convince the judges, what they took note of was "that these men had been with Jesus."—Acts 4:13. I would like to think that the first impression received from an Apostle would be "that person has been with Jesus." Apostle Paul said it best I think and I borrow from his teachings when I choose for myself, "while they might be an Apostle unto others, they will not be unto me." Character comes first. Matthew 23:11 states, "But he that is greatest among you shall be your servant." So yes, Patient Endurance is one of the noteworthy qualifiers of true Apostles. This was also a very admirable quality in the life of Esther as she prepared to take on the most dangerous assignment.

Apostles Must Have Patience

[15]Jesus instructed the Apostles in Luke 21:19 "to possess their souls in patience". The backdrop of this instruction was to be one of immense persecution, betrayal by friends and close relatives, hatred and martyrdom. With all these frightful things prophesied in the Apostles' future, Jesus strategy for them to successfully navigate through this time was by means of patience.

Patience would be the key to the Apostles remaining in control and directing their own souls. Jesus prophesied that they would be beaten in the synagogues and hauled before rulers and Kings and subjected to great injustice. Their challenge during their upcoming trials, as they stood before these men, who had the power and the desire to persecute them as we read in Luke 21:12, would be to consistently demonstrate the character of Christ in their thoughts, attitudes and responses, firstly toward God; then to themselves and toward their persecutors.

Persecution is possibly the most potent and successful weapon satan has been deploying against all of mankind for centuries. He has had more than millennia to observe our makeup and implement his machinations, and has become expert in its use. The thing that has made persecution such a powerful strategy for the enemy is that it portends to result in the two things that men fear most: pain and loss.

Pain and loss, when allowed to work in our flesh unchecked, provide the enemy with the access he desires to our souls. It provides him with the leverage he requires to shift us from our position of completing God's purposes in the earth, to one of despair, destruction and ultimately loss of our reward. The enemy's strategic application of pain and loss has caused many a Believer to abandon themselves to angry malicious thoughts, outrage, pride, retaliation, self-pity and ultimately blasphemy—Job 1:11 "*But extend your hand and strike everything he has, and he will no doubt curse you to your face!*" [Italicized]

15 From Michael Haynes, one of the Pastoral Ministers at Dominion-Life International Ministries.

Toward the early Apostles satan would throw his full arsenal including darts of persecution and trials. These trials included pain from beatings and torture, pain from betrayal and loss of relationships, pain from imprisonment and banishment, pain from abandonment and humiliation and the ultimate pain of death. Jesus prophetically gave the Apostles a glimpse into what they would face,—Luke 21:12—and the reason they would have to face it. He also showed them the result that Heaven expected out of it. Jesus expected that during their trials and persecution, they would produce "testimonies"—Luke 21:13. He expected that, in spite of and through their afflictions, they would be able to be effective witnesses of the truth of the gospel to everyone they met.

There was to be no forethought, no planning, and no rehearsal of a defence on their part. The natural fleshly reactions that the enemy pressures us to release in times like these were to be kept in check. The Apostles were to present themselves to the Holy Spirit, without any agenda, and without a defence or exit strategy. They would need to possess their souls throughout the ordeal in order for the Holy Spirit to execute God's purpose through them.

But even in those trying times Jesus did not leave them without an example. Before they were required to endure their own trials, Jesus went through it all, before their very eyes, and by the Holy Spirit, imprinted on their souls what it would take for them to succeed. Jesus was despised and rejected of men (Isaiah 53:3), was falsely accused and did not defend Himself—Isaiah 53:7,—and endured the ultimate injustice of a criminal's death on the cross—Hebrews 12:2. He became their blueprint, and their patient endurance would allow them to interpret and execute God's plans from it.

Patience is translated from the Greek word "*hupomone*", which means possessing a cheerful or hopeful endurance and constancy, specifically during trials. It is derived from the root word "*hupomeno*", which means to endure. Patience was the ingredient that allowed Jesus to successfully navigate the cross, and is the essential ingredient working in us to empower us to deny ourselves and take up our cross. Hebrews 12:2 says: "keeping our eyes fixed on Jesus, the Pioneer and Perfecter of our faith. For the joy set out for Him He *endured* (*hupomeno*) the cross, disregarding its shame, and *has taken His seat at the right hand of the Throne* of God".

The writer of Hebrews compares the Believer's life to a race—Hebrews 12:1-3. He did not mean a sprint, which requires speed over a short duration. In sprints, athletes expend their energy in a burst, over a short time, and without a great concern for endurance. However, the race he refers to can be seen as a marathon. The Greek word used for race is "*agona*" from which we derive the word agony. It is also translated as "conflict" and "contention"—Colossians 2:21; 1 Thessalonians 2:2. So we understand from its usage, that the type of race being described requires a tremendous struggle and effort from the participants. And so the Believer's life is not to be considered a walk in the park, but a gruelling fight to the finish.

As marathon runners will tell you, the most significant struggle they face is not from the other participants, or from a hostile environment. Those are realities that the runner has little control over, and the writer in Hebrews also never mentions the presence of others in the race, nor does he describe the immediate environment. The great conflict or the agony of the race the athlete experiences, is the struggle that takes place on the inside, and the writer in Hebrews parallels this to weights that we must lay aside, and the sin that can easily beset us—Hebrews 12:1.

This internal struggle in the athlete manifests itself as the greatest challenge the runner faces in the race, and is something referred to as "hitting the wall". "The wall" usually comes at a critical stage of a marathon between the 20th to 22nd mile of a 26 mile race. The wall hits the athlete as a sudden onset of fatigue and loss of energy that threatens to end the race for him/her. It is at this point the runner has to make a crucial decision whether to receive replenishment and press through to the end, or quit the race. The thing that enables the runner to break through the wall and finish the race is Endurance. Our Lord Jesus faced His wall in the garden of Gethsemane: Mark 14:32-36

> "Then they came to a place which was named Gethsemane; and He said to His disciples, "Sit here while I pray." 33 And He took Peter, James, and John with Him, and He began to be troubled and deeply distressed. 34 Then He said to them, "My soul is exceedingly sorrowful, even to death. Stay here and

> watch." 35 He went a little farther, and fell on the ground, and prayed that if it were possible, the hour might pass from Him.
> 36 And He said, "Abba, Father, all things are possible for You. Take this cup away from Me; nevertheless, not what I will, but what You will."

It was at this point, His strength left Him. His soul was deeply grieved, to the point of dying. It was sheer agony for Him. And, it was at this crucial point, He received replenishment, just like a marathon runner does, and He was able to possess His soul—Luke 22:42-44.

> "Saying, Father, if thou be willing, remove this cup from me: nevertheless not my will, but thine, be done. 43 And there appeared an angel unto him from heaven, strengthening him.
> 44 And being in an agony he prayed more earnestly: and his sweat was as it were great drops of blood falling down to the ground." KJV

Never before was it recorded in Scripture that our Lord had felt this way. There was no experience from His past, which He could draw on to prepare Him for this time. It was a critical stage. However, He was able to press through the wall that separated Him from His destiny and that threatened to derail His purpose. He took hold of His soul, endured the agony, and completed the will of God—Hebrews 5:7-9.

> "During his earthly life Christ offered both requests and supplications, with loud cries and tears, to the one who was able to save him from death and he was heard because of his devotion. 8 Although he was a son, he learned obedience through the things he suffered. 9 And by being perfected in this way, he became the source of eternal salvation to all who obey him," NET

By patiently enduring the suffering of pressing through His wall, Jesus learned obedience. He was perfected or completed, and became the source of eternal salvation for everyone, which was the ultimate plan of the Father. With this image of Jesus imprinted on their hearts by the Holy Spirit, the Apostles would derive the technology to breakthrough their "walls". The Apostle Paul would later write in his letter to the Philippians—Philippians 2:5-8!

> "Let this mind be in you, which was also in Christ Jesus: 6 Who, being in the form of God, thought it not robbery to be equal with God: 7 But made himself of no reputation, and took upon him the form of a servant, and was made in the likeness of men: 8 And being found in fashion as a man, he humbled himself, and became obedient unto death, even the death of the cross." NET

Jesus disarmed satan of his most potent weapons at Gethsemane and at Calvary. By securing eternal salvation, Jesus procured a magnificent future for all who believes in Him. No longer would the enemy be able to destabilize the Apostles as he did with Peter at the crucifixion by using the threat of pain and loss of life. From that point on, the Apostles and all who believe on Jesus, have been given a hope that compensates for all they might lose through suffering and trials brought about by the enemy. They have the hope of a blessing, which multiplies and replaces everything satan tries to take away, and also provides an eternity for us to enjoy it—2 Corinthians 4:7-18.

> "But we have this treasure in clay jars, so that the extraordinary power belongs to God and does not come from us. 8 We are experiencing trouble on every side, but are not crushed; we are perplexed, but not driven to despair; 9 we are persecuted, but not abandoned; we are knocked down, but not destroyed, 10 always carrying around in our body the death of Jesus, so that the life of Jesus may also be made visible in our body. 11 For we who are alive are constantly being handed over to death for Jesus' sake, so that the life of Jesus may also be made visible in our mortal body. 12 As a result, death is at work in us, but life is at work in you. 13 But since we have the same spirit of faith as that shown in what has been written, "*I believed; therefore I spoke*," we also believe, therefore we also speak. 14 We do so because we know that the one who raised

up Jesus will also raise us up with Jesus and will bring us with you into his presence. 15 For all these things are for your sake, so that the grace that is including more and more people may cause thanksgiving to increase to the glory of God. 16 Therefore we do not despair, but even if our physical body is wearing away, our inner person is being renewed day by day. 17 For our momentary, light suffering is producing for us an eternal weight of glory far beyond all comparison 18 because we are not looking at what can be seen but at what cannot be seen. For what can be seen is temporary, but what cannot be seen is eternal." NET

"And Peter said, "Look, we have left everything we own to follow you!" 29 Then Jesus said to them, "I tell you the truth, there is no one who has left home or wife or brothers or parents or children for the sake of God's kingdom 30 who will not receive many times more in this age—and in the age to come, eternal life." Luke 18:28-30 NET

"Then Peter said to him, "Look, we have left everything to follow you! What then will there be for us?" 28 Jesus said to them, "I tell you the truth: In the age when all things are renewed, when the Son of Man sits on his glorious throne, you who have followed me will also sit on twelve thrones, judging the twelve tribes of Israel. 29 And whoever has left houses or brothers or sisters or father or mother or children or fields for my sake will receive a hundred times as much and will inherit eternal life." Mathew 19:27-29 NET

However, the Apostles understood, that despite the great and precious promises made available to them, that the key to accessing the promise, which came at the end of their trials, was endurance. Without the ability to endure to the end, there would be no prize. Just like in the case of a marathon runner, without patient endurance through the "gruelling stages" there is no victory—Matthew 10:22.

> "But remember the former days when you endured a harsh conflict of suffering after you were enlightened. 33 At times you were publicly exposed to abuse and afflictions, and at other times you came to share with others who were treated in that way. 34 For in fact you shared the sufferings of those in prison, and you accepted the confiscation of your belongings with joy, because you knew that you certainly had a better and lasting possession. 35 So do not throw away your confidence, because it has great reward. 36 For you need endurance in order to do God's will and so receive what is promised. 37 For *just a little longer* and *he who is coming will arrive and not delay. But my righteous one will live by faith, and if he shrinks back, I take no pleasure in him*. But we are not among those who shrink back and thus perish, but are among those who have faith and preserve their souls." Hebrews 10:32-39 NET

In Hebrews 12:1-3; James 1:4 we see four dimensions of apostolic grace that can become ours through the technology of patience!

> "Therefore we also, since we are surrounded by so great a cloud of witnesses, let us lay aside every weight, and the sin which so easily ensnares us, and let us run with endurance the race that is set before us, 2 looking unto Jesus, the author and finisher of our faith, who for the joy that was set before Him endured the cross, despising the shame, and has sat down at the right hand of the throne of God. 3 For consider Him who endured such hostility from sinners against Himself, lest you become weary and discouraged in your souls."

> "But let patience have its perfect work, that you may be perfect and complete, lacking nothing."

1. The Ability To Decode The Plans Of God: Patience allows us to decode and apply the blueprint for God's plan for our lives, which is to rooted and built up in Christ—Colossians 2:7 and to be conformed to Christ—Romans 12:2. This is expressed in James 1:4 as us being "perfect and complete and not

deficient". Patience, when allowed to work in us, completes the work of God in building us up into Christ, both individually and corporately as the Body of Christ.

2. Finishing Ability: In Hebrews 12:2, Patience (endurance) is what enabled Jesus to become the "finisher of the faith". It is the key to finishing the work God has given us, and to not become ruined by the schemes of the enemy. The enemy often uses a 3-step descending ladder to erect a wall in our life to derail us. These steps are:
    a. Mumbling within ourselves!
    b. Complaining to others!
    c. Open rebellion against the purposes of God!

   However, patience keeps us constantly on track!
3. Ability To Persevere: Patience gives us the ability to persevere by taking away the "sting of the trial or persecution", which is pain and the suffering of loss! It also offers us the opportunity to acquire something much more valuable than what we will lose.
    - Patience guarantees maturity and conformity to the character of Christ—James 1:2.
    - You will be rewarded and receive the tender mercies of God—James 5:11.
    - Patience is needed to attain the promise—Hebrews 10:36.
4. Maintain Focus: Patient endurance allows us to keep our focus on the goal of God's purpose and run the race in spite of obstacles—Hebrews 10:36.

Jesus understood that His temporary loss would result in His ultimate gain. We also learn through patient endurance, as Job did, that God is tender and merciful and will remove the sting of loss, and bless us in the end. Patience is a vital part of the process that enables God to work over a long span of time, if needed, to produce in us the image of Christ so that we "may be perfect and complete, lacking nothing"—James 1:4.

4TH Attitude: We Must Have An Understanding That This Is Our Day—The Third Day.

It is a time set in the plans of God. We must see that we have "come for such a time as this"—Esther 4:14. But notice clearly, it was on the third day that Esther went in to see the king, Esther 5:1. Timing is every bit as important as the cause. It is when time and purpose come together that you achieve the goal. Jesus was born in the fullness of time, Galatians 4:4. There is a time for everything as stated in Ecclesiastes 3:1.

There is much in Scripture regarding the "Third Day" and it will augur well for us to explore a few; Luke 13:32 says: "And He said to them, "Go, tell that fox, 'Behold, I cast out demons and perform cures today and tomorrow, and the third day I shall be perfected."

- The Earth Was Created—Genesis 1:9-13.
- Abraham's Ultimate Test—Genesis 22:1-5.
- God's Major Appearing To All Of Israel—Exodus 19:9-11.
- Saul's Death Was Announced—2 Samuel 1:1-4.
- The Rebuilding Of The Temple Was Finished—Ezra 6:14-15a.
- Esther Put On Her Royal Apparel And Found The King's Favour—Esther 5:1-2.
- Jesus Was Launched Into His Ministry Of Miracles, Water Was Turned Into Wine—John 2:1-11.
- Jesus Rose Again From The Dead—Matthew 16:21; Acts 10:38-41.

5TH Attitude: We Must Expect The King To Put Out His Sceptre And Grant Us Favour—Esther 5:2-3.

This is a season of the favour of God. We are not talking about a few acts of favour granted to an undeserving people. There is no sacrifice on God's part to do something good for us. This kind of favour is a condition, not an act! Just as Mary was highly favoured and Jesus walked in favour with God and man so too is the Church to accept its condition as favoured also with God and man! It has been said that a sure way to get what you ask for is to expect nothing and thus you will get exactly what you expected, nothing. We beloved must change our expectation levels to agree with our condition as favoured of God.

CHAPTER FIVE

PRESENT TRUTH

Present Truth was the terminology used by the Apostle Peter to describe the revelation of Jesus Christ at that time. In 2 Peter 1:12 he writes: "For this reason I will not be negligent to remind you always of these things, though you know and are established in the present truth." Apostle Peter reminded the Saints to continue to operate within the context of the current revelation they were receiving from God. In this particular passage of Scripture the Apostle Peter was warning the Saints that false-teachers and erroneous doctrine would and do arise, even though they were very much in touch with what the Lord was speaking to the Church at that time. It is from this premise we have coined the same phrase and applied the term Present Truth to the Church, as we know it.

Present Truth then, is a term that has been coined to speak to the current revelation that God is releasing on earth through the ministry of His Apostles and Prophets. God operates by seasons of activity and for every season, He provides the spiritual resource for that season in the form of revelation.

A real-time building project has different stages added on at different times throughout the duration of the project. Likewise, Christ is building His Church, and the purpose of present truth revelation is to provide the necessary building elements through revelation knowledge. They are needed for the Church to shape its mentalities, behavioural patterns, character, and modes of operation.

Present Truth is also a term that we use to communicate the present process of revelation that currently defines the course of our spiritual experience. The purpose of present truth or current revelation from God is not so that we build denominations or moves of God around them, but that we become transformed according to that revelation.

The Church illustrated in the Book of Acts was very powerful, alive, progressive Spirit-filled, Spirit-directed Church. However, during the Dark Ages a church arose that was very much a shadow of the Church seen in the Book of Acts. Most of the Five-Fold Ministry callings as outlined in Ephesians 4:11 "And He Himself gave some to be apostles, some prophets, some evangelists, and some pastors and some teachers. For the equipping of the saints for the work of the ministry, for the edifying of the body of Christ"—had disappeared from within the structure of the visible Church, the Body of Believers in Jesus Christ.

It was not until in the early 1500's when the Roman Catholic priest named Martin Luther, uncovered a very pivotal present truth as he translated the Scriptures into the everyday common language. Luther discovered Romans 1:17b "...But the righteous shall live by faith." ASV. This impacted Luther so much that he risked his entire existence within the Catholic Church by opposing the erroneous teachings of Rome. His actions sparked the Reformation, which totally changed Christendom of that day and in fact it is still in effect to this day.

Time and time again down through history, we have seen present truth after present truth being established to the Body of Christ.

- The 1500s saw the Holy Spirit move upon Martin Luther to stand up against the ills of his day and declare the Word of God, without compromise.
- In the 1600's water baptism returned to the Body of Believers. Thank God for that truth being restored to the Body, as we practice it today without any contradiction.

- The 1700's saw holiness and sanctification restored. At that time tremendous revelation was revealed concerning our sanctification and ability to live holy lives.
- With the 1880's came the restored truth on divine faith healing. We thank God for this truth, as it has found its place forever in the Church of Jesus Christ in the earth. We can walk in divine health; we can believe the Lord for healing and, He has proven Himself repeatedly in this dimension, as many Saints have been healed.
- At the turn of the 20th Century there was a tremendous truth restored to the Body of Christ regarding the baptism of the Holy Spirit and speaking with other tongues. This I believe was one of the most powerful moves of the Spirit of God, as we saw major "Pentecostal" denominations and several independent groups rising all over the earth proclaiming a bold new Faith that changed the face of the Church at that time.
- In the 1940's we saw the restoration of the laying on of hands and personal prophecy return on the scene.
- The 1950's returned praise and worship and body ministry (where the Saints would minister to each other), with dancing. During this time, deliverance and evangelism also became prevalent within the Body of Christ.
- In the 1960's, the local church fully began to understand demon possession and the effects it has on people in every walk of life. For a long time this had been dismissed as a paranormal occurrence, but during this time, the Church gained insight into the reality of demons and demonic activity and with that insight came tremendous release and freedom for peoples from all walks of life.
- In the early 1970's, the emphasis was on discipleship, family life and Church growth. In the mid to late 1970's, Believers were taught that the Word of God also contained deep teachings on faith, along with prosperity and Word teachings.
- In the early 1980's we saw powerful revelation being released on the Kingdom of God and our dominion in Christ. This revealed to us our place as kings and priest unto God and gave us the power of declaration.

- In the late 1980's and early 1990's came the restoration of Prophets to the Body of Christ. With this move we saw the full restoration of modern day Prophets back to the Body of Christ.
- Beginning in the late 1990's we began seeing the restoration of Apostles to the Body of Christ and this continues even today. There is such a tremendous awareness of the government of God in the earth. It is producing boldness and the wisdom in God's people to stand strong for the Lord, regardless of adversities.

As we continue in our quest to see the Church of Jesus Christ become mature in this generation and ensure that the next generation be equipped correctly to continue the advance of the Kingdom of God in the earth, there are more "present truths" being revealed to us. With every previous "present truth" that was released to the Body of Christ there has been tremendous battles for it to be accepted, and it is no different today. Here are a few examples:

Jesus Christ coming to fulfil the requirements of the Old Covenant and establish the New Covenant was resisted by the leaders of the Old Covenant system every step of the way. His fight has been well documented in the Scriptures. However, I believe that the following truly sums up His battle for a then "present truth" to be released into the earth.

We know that God's interaction with planet earth began with a Covenant in the Garden of Eden with Adam and Eve, who messed up and had to be expelled. God then began a journey to restore that initial Covenant He made with man by the sending of His Only Begotten Son to die and pay the ultimate price for the sins of the world. However, before His arrival we had several other Covenants, all-leading up to the final and most comprehensive of them all, The New Covenant, which we now enjoy.

This is important to understand because of the fact that in Adam all died. When the first man (Adam) and woman (Eve) sinned in the Garden of Eden, they broke God's Covenant with mankind; the entire human race became guilty of that act. This is so because Adam and Eve only began reproducing after their fallen state and God had to secure a lineage for the eventual birth of His Son into the earth so that He could become the "last Adam", not the last Moses or the last Abraham or the last Israel; but the "last Adam".

> "And so it is written, "The first man Adam became a living being." The last Adam became a life-giving spirit. 46 However, the spiritual is not first, but the natural, and afterward the spiritual. 47 The first man was of the earth, made of dust; the second Man is the Lord from heaven. 48 As was the man of dust, so also are those who are made of dust; and as is the heavenly Man, so also are those who are heavenly. 49 And as we have borne the image of the man of dust, we shall also bear the image of the heavenly Man." 1 Corinthians 15:45-49 NASB

Understanding The Covenants

From the fall of man and the breaking of that initial Covenant in the Garden of Eden, God began His search for a new man. In doing so there were several Covenants that were made, as can be seen through at least six major Covenants (seven if we were to consider the Adamic Covenant as having Two Covenants) recorded in Scripture, which are as follows:

The Adamic Covenant

[16]The Adamic Covenant can be thought of in two parts: the Edenic Covenant (innocence) and the Adamic Covenant (grace). The Edenic Covenant is found in Genesis 1:26-30, 2:16-17.

> "Then God said, "Let Us make man in Our image, according to Our likeness; let them have dominion over the fish of the sea, over the birds of the air, and over the cattle, over all the earth and over every creeping thing that creeps on the earth." 27 So God created man in His own image; in the image of God He created him; male and female He created them. 28 Then God blessed them, and God said to them, "Be fruitful and multiply; fill the earth and subdue it; have dominion over the fish of the

16 Researched at Got Questions Ministries

> sea, over the birds of the air, and over every living thing that moves on the earth." 29 And God said, "See, I have given you every herb that yields seed which is on the face of all the earth, and every tree whose fruit yields seed; to you it shall be for food. 30 Also, to every beast of the earth, to every bird of the air, and to everything that creeps on the earth, in which there is life, I have given every green herb for food"; and it was so"
>
> "And the Lord God commanded the man, saying, "Of every tree of the garden you may freely eat; 17 but of the tree of the knowledge of good and evil you shall not eat, for in the day that you eat of it you shall surely die."

The Adamic Covenant is found in Genesis 3:16-19: "To the woman He said: "I will greatly multiply your sorrow and your conception; In pain you shall bring forth children; Your desire shall be for your husband, And he shall rule over you." 17 Then to Adam He said, "Because you have heeded the voice of your wife, and have eaten from the tree of which I commanded you, saying, 'You shall not eat of it': "Cursed is the ground for your sake; In toil you shall eat of it All the days of your life. 18 Both thorns and thistles it shall bring forth for you, And you shall eat the herb of the field. 19 In the sweat of your face you shall eat bread Till you return to the ground, For out of it you were taken; For dust you are, And to dust you shall return." Included in this Covenant are the curses pronounced against mankind for the sin of Adam and Eve, as well as God's provision for that sin (Genesis 3:15). As the result of Adam's sin, the following curses were pronounced:

- Enmity between satan and Eve and her descendants.
- Painful childbirth for women.
- Marital strife.
- The soil cursed.
- Introduction of thorns and thistles.
- Survival to be a struggle.
- Death introduced.
- Death will be the inescapable fate of all living things.

The Noahic Covenant

The Noahic Covenant was an unconditional Covenant between God and Noah (specifically) and humanity (generally—Genesis 9). God gave the rainbow as the sign of the Covenant, a promise that the entire earth would never again flood and a reminder that God can and will judge sin—2 Peter 2:5 "For if God did not spare the angels who sinned, but cast them down to hell and delivered them into chains of darkness, to be reserved for judgment; 5 and did not spare the ancient world, but saved Noah, one of eight people, a preacher of righteousness, bringing in the flood on the world of the ungodly."

> "Then God spoke to Noah and to his sons with him, saying: 9 "And as for Me, behold, I establish My covenant with you and with your descendants after you, 10 and with every living creature that is with you: the birds, the cattle, and every beast of the earth with you, of all that go out of the ark, every beast of the earth. 11 Thus I establish My covenant with you: Never again shall all flesh be cut off by the waters of the flood; never again shall there be a flood to destroy the earth." 12 And God said: "This is the sign of the covenant which I make between Me and you, and every living creature that is with you, for perpetual generations: 13 I set My rainbow in the cloud, and it shall be for the sign of the covenant between Me and the earth. 14 It shall be, when I bring a cloud over the earth, that the rainbow shall be seen in the cloud; 15 and I will remember My covenant which is between Me and you and every living creature of all flesh; the waters shall never again become a flood to destroy all flesh. 16 The rainbow shall be in the cloud, and I will look on it to remember the everlasting covenant between God and every living creature of all flesh that is on the earth." 17 And God said to Noah, "This is the sign of the covenant which I have established between Me and all flesh that is on the earth."

The Abrahamic Covenant

The Abrahamic Covenant is recorded in Genesis 12:1-3, 6-7, 13:14-17, 15, 17:1-14, 22:15-18. In this Covenant, God promised many things to Abraham. He personally promised that He would make Abraham's name great—Genesis 12:2 "I will make you a great nation; I will bless you And make your name great; And you shall be a blessing." God also promised that Abraham would have numerous physical descendents—Genesis 13:16 "And I will make your descendants as the dust of the earth; so that if a man could number the dust of the earth, then your descendants also could be numbered." And that he would be the father of a multitude of nations—Genesis 17:1-7 "When Abram was ninety-nine years old, the Lord appeared to Abram and said to him, "I am Almighty God; walk before Me and be blameless. 2 And I will make My covenant between Me and you, and will multiply you exceedingly." 3 Then Abram fell on his face, and God talked with him, saying: 4 "As for Me, behold, My covenant is with you, and you shall be a father of many nations. 5 No longer shall your name be called Abram, but your name shall be Abraham; for I have made you a father of many nations. 6 I will make you exceedingly fruitful; and I will make nations of you, and kings shall come from you. 7 And I will establish My covenant between Me and you and your descendants after you in their generations, for an everlasting covenant, to be God to you and your descendants after you."

Most of what are called the Old Testament Scriptures record God's dealings with His chosen earthly nation, Israel. In the book of Genesis we read of how God made a covenant with Abraham. This Abrahamic covenant was reaffirmed to Abraham's son, Isaac, and then to Isaac's son, Jacob, who became Israel.

The Mosaic Covenant

The Mosaic Covenant is found in Deuteronomy 11 revealing that part of the Mosaic Covenant was the Ten Commandments—(Exodus 20) and the rest of the Law, which contained over 600 commands, roughly 300 positive and 300 negative. The Mosaic Covenant was centred around God's giving of His Divine Law to Moses on Mount Sinai. The

Mosaic Covenant is especially significant because in it God promises to make Israel "a kingdom of priests and a holy nation"—Exodus 19:6. Israel was to be God's light to the dark world around them. They were to be a separate and called-out nation so that everyone around them would know that they worshiped Yahweh, the covenant-keeping God. It is significant because it is here that Israel received the Mosaic Law that was to be a schoolmaster pointing the way towards the coming of Christ—Galatians 3:24-25. The Mosaic Law would reveal to people their sinfulness and their need for a Saviour, and it is the Mosaic Law that Christ Himself said that He did not come to abolish but to fulfil. This is an important point because some people get confused by thinking that keeping the Law saved people in the Old Testament, but the Bible is clear that salvation has always been by faith alone, and the promise of salvation by faith that God had made to Abraham as part of the Abrahamic Covenant still remained in effect—Galatians 3:16-18.

Also, the sacrificial system of the *Mosaic Covenant* did not really take away sins—Hebrews 10:1-4; it simply foreshadowed the bearing of sin by Christ, the perfect High Priest who was also the Perfect Sacrifice—Hebrews 9:11-28. Therefore, the *Mosaic Covenant* itself, with all its detailed laws, could not save people. It is not that there was any problem with the Law itself, for the Law is perfect and was given by a Holy God, but the Law had no power to give people new life, and the people were not able to obey the Law perfectly—Galatians 3:21.

The Mosaic Covenant is also referred to as the Old Covenant (2 Corinthians 3:14; Hebrews 8:6, 13) and as replaced by the *New Covenant* in Christ (Luke 22:20; 1 Corinthians 11:25; 2 Corinthians 3:6; Hebrews 8:8; 8:13; 9:15; 12:24).

The Davidic Covenant

The Davidic Covenant amplifies the "seed" aspect of the Abrahamic Covenant—2 Samuel 7:8-16. The promises to David in this passage are significant. God promised that David's lineage would last forever and that his kingdom would never pass away permanently.

> "Now therefore, thus shall you say to My servant David, 'Thus says the Lord of hosts: "I took you from the sheepfold, from

> following the sheep, to be ruler over My people, over Israel.
> 9 And I have been with you wherever you have gone, and have cut off all your enemies from before you, and have made you a great name, like the name of the great men who are on the earth. 10 Moreover I will appoint a place for My people Israel, and will plant them, that they may dwell in a place of their own and move no more; nor shall the sons of wickedness oppress them anymore, as previously, 11 since the time that I commanded judges to be over My people Israel, and have caused you to rest from all your enemies. Also the Lord tells you that He will make you a house. 12 "When your days are fulfilled and you rest with your fathers, I will set up your seed after you, who will come from your body, and I will establish his kingdom. 13 He shall build a house for My name, and I will establish the throne of his kingdom forever. 14 I will be his Father, and he shall be My son. If he commits iniquity, I will chasten him with the rod of men and with the blows of the sons of men. 15 But My mercy shall not depart from him, as I took it from Saul, whom I removed from before you. 16 And your house and your kingdom shall be established forever before you. Your throne shall be established forever."

However, we know that these Covenants had a spiritual significance to them. In the Old Testament God made a Covenant to Abraham declaring to him that in his seed all the nations of the earth would be blessed. And we know that seed mentioned in the Old Testament referred to Isaac, the promised son. However, we also know that after the coming of the Messiah (Jesus Christ) and His death and resurrection revealed that Abraham's seed was not referring to Isaac, but to Jesus Christ—Galatians Chapter 4. We have to also understand that when the Old Testament declares that Jesus Christ would sit on the throne of His ancestor David; it was not referring to an earthly throne but a spiritual throne, because the Kingdom of God is NOT a physical kingdom of this earth! These are very important things to know and remember!

So after all of these Covenants, Jesus Christ the promised Messiah came to earth, came to His chosen people, the Jews and they did not receive Him. He goes on to not only fulfil all the requirements of the Old Covenant, but He declared to the Jews that the strength of the Old Covenant would be completely destroyed.

As is know the strength or symbol of the Old Covenant was the Temple, where the God of Israel and the whole earth chose to live. Jesus Christ came to the earth fully knowing that He came to die and to rise from the dead in order to establish The New Covenant in His Blood. Knowing this, He made the following announcement to His Disciples concerning the Temple, which was the strength and symbol of the Old Covenant—Matthew 24:1-2.

> "Then Jesus went out and departed from the temple, and His disciples came up to show Him the buildings of the temple.
> 2 And Jesus said to them, "Do you not see all these things? Assuredly, I say to you, not *one* stone shall be left here upon another, that shall not be thrown down."

The New Covenant

The New Covenant recorded in the Old Testament is one that was not made in the Old Testament times but was only prophesied and foretold in the Old Testament Scriptures. The great Old Testament Prophet who prophesied the establishment of the New Covenant was Jeremiah whom God gave the revelation to. Hence Jesus Christ came to fulfil the Old and establish the New Covenant and for the Jews that was a major "*Present Truth*".

> "Behold, the days are coming, says the LORD, when I will make a new covenant with the house of Israel and with the house of Judah—32 not according to the covenant that I made with their fathers in the day *that* I took them by the hand to lead them out of the land of Egypt, My covenant which they broke, though I was a husband to them, says the LORD. 33 But this *is* the covenant that I will make with the house of Israel after those days, says the LORD: I will put My law in their minds, and write it on their hearts; and I will be their God, and they shall be My people. 34 No more shall every man teach his neighbour,

> and every man his brother, saying, 'Know the Lord,' for they all shall know Me, from the least of them to the greatest of them, says the Lord. For I will forgive their iniquity, and their sin I will remember no more." Jeremiah 31:31-34

> "But now He has obtained a more excellent ministry, inasmuch as He is also Mediator of a better covenant, which was established on better promises. 7 For if that first *covenant* had been faultless, then no place would have been sought for a second. 8 Because finding fault with them, He says: "Behold, the days are coming, says the Lord, when I will make a new covenant with the house of Israel and with the house of Judah—9 not according to the covenant that I made with their fathers in the day when I took them by the hand to lead them out of the land of Egypt; because they did not continue in My covenant, and I disregarded them, says the Lord. 10 For this *is* the covenant that I will make with the house of Israel after those days, says the Lord: I will put My laws in their mind and write them on their hearts; and I will be their God, and they shall be My people. 11 None of them shall teach his neighbour, and none his brother, saying, 'Know the Lord,' for all shall know Me, from the least of them to the greatest of them. 12 For I will be merciful to their unrighteousness, and their sins and their lawless deeds I will remember no more." 13 In that He says, "A new *covenant*," He has made the first obsolete. Now what is becoming obsolete and growing old is ready to vanish away." Hebrews 8:6-13

Another major "*Present Truth*" that occurred in the First Century church was the idea of Gentiles being on the same level as Jews in the sight of God.

> "For this reason I, Paul, the prisoner of Christ Jesus for you Gentiles—2 f indeed you have heard of the dispensation of the grace of God which was given to me for you, 3 *how that by revelation He made known to me the mystery* [as I have briefly written already, 4 by which, when you read, you may

> understand my knowledge in the mystery of Christ], 5 *which in other ages was not made known to the sons of men, as it has now been revealed by the Spirit to His holy apostles and prophets: 6 that the Gentiles should be fellow heirs, of the same body, and partakers of His promise in Christ through the gospel*, 7 of which I became a minister according to the gift of the grace of God given to me by the effective working of His power." [Italics added] Ephesians 3:1-7

That was a vey hard "pill" to swallow for many of the First Century Jews, that the Gentiles were fellow heirs of the same Body and partakers of Gospel—that they were saved.

Not only that but the fact that this was now being told to them by a former Jew, none other than the Apostle Paul (formerly Saul).

In the next chapter it would be beneficial for us to spend some time dealing with Matthew Chapter 24 and some of the misconceptions that have been taught over the years. For some of you it will be "*Present Truth*" and every fibre in your being may seek to resist it, but let me encourage reading through to the end, with your Bibles in hand.

Chapter Six

Understanding Matthew Chapter 24

As we seek to build the Church that Jesus Christ referred to in Matthew Chapter 16, it is absolutely important that we get our Eschatology correct. Eschatology refers to the study of end-times. We know that He is using the Five-Fold Ministry Gifts of Apostles, Prophets, Evangelists, Pastors and Teachers to fulfil the task of building the Church, as recorded in Ephesians 4:11-16:

> "And he gave some, apostles; and some, prophets; and some, evangelists; and some, pastors and teachers; 12 For the perfecting of the saints, for the work of the ministry, for the edifying of the body of Christ: 13 Till we all come in the unity of the faith, and of the knowledge of the Son of God, unto a perfect man, unto the measure of the stature of the fullness of Christ: 14 That we henceforth be no more children, tossed to and fro, and carried about with every wind of doctrine, by the sleight of men, and cunning craftiness, whereby they lie in wait to deceive; 15 But speaking the truth in love, may grow up into him in all things, which is the head, even Christ: 16 From whom the whole body fitly joined together and compacted

by that which every joint supplieth, according to the effectual working in the measure of every part, maketh increase of the body unto the edifying of itself in love." KJV

As we launch into this study one of the things that I believe and understand is this: We cannot keep living our lives as Christians with an exclusive, futuristic, mindset where every thing in Scripture is still to be fulfilled.

I believe that part of the anointing and expectation of Apostles and Prophets is to decode the mysteries of Scripture and to also reveal what has already come to pass. In this and the next chapter I will offer some insights as to what I, and many other Apostles believe have already taken place.

I believe that how we understand and view life and the times in which we live will dictate how we build. In essence if we have an incorrect Eschatology we would place emphasis on the wrong things and thereby build inaccurately.

For example we have had untold numbers of inaccurate and false prophecies concerning the end of the world and the return of Jesus Christ, all because of a misinterpretation of Scripture. As such many untold numbers of people have sold their houses and lands and valuables, and have been swindled out of their money and property all because of an incorrect belief system. And yet with all the false prophecies that have come and gone and with the many more that will come, Christians are not studying the Scriptures to come to a sensible and accurate understanding of the "end-times"... This must change. We must have wise, master builders who can correctly discern and interpret the Word of God so that we can live accurate and sensible lives. In this book we are seeking to do just that!

Of all the teachings concerning the "end-times" in the earth today, none is more controversial and misunderstood as to what is recorded in Matthew Chapter 24. As such I believe that if we are to be successful in building a Present Truth Church in the earth we must revisit a lot of the misconceptions and misguided teachings and beliefs that have arisen out of that Chapter. We need to seek truth and clarify things so that we can build accurately.

Matthew Chapter 24—A Closer Look!

In this section I would like to share with you from one of the best books that I have read on Eschatology—"Victorious Eschatology"—written by Harold Eberle and Martin Trench. The following excerpt is from chapter one of that book.

We are looking at what the Scriptures really have to say concerning the "end-times" as we seek to have an accurate Eschatology... There is just so much error and false prophecies concerning the end of all things going around that we need to have a correct understanding of this...

Eschatology refers to the study of end-times. The Eschatological view that I believe the Bible speaks about shows that the Kingdom of God will grow and advance until it fills the earth. The Church will rise in unity, maturity, and glory before the return of Jesus. I also believe that Scripture presents to us an Eschatology that is Victorious.

As we go into this study of Matthew Chapter 24 here are a few things that I would like for us to fully understand:

1. The New Testament was written to the Jews to signal the *end* to the Old Covenant and the establishment of the New!
2. The New Testament was also written to the 1st Century Believers as to how the New Nation called The Church should live in relation to Almighty God!
3. That the Scripture in it's original content had no Chapters and Verse and was placed there by the translators of the original manuscripts.
4. That the Old Testament completely and totally came to an end around AD 70 and was replaced by a New Covenant (The New Testament), which is referred to as an Everlasting Covenant.
5. That there is no reference whatsoever pointing to another Covenant to come!

One of the most amazing studies of the Covenants is of the Eschatology of the Covenants. The word "Eschatology" means: "Any system of doctrines concerning last, or final, matters". The word comes from the Greek word "E*schato", meaning: "last". So it is the study of those things, which are to occur last, the things that come* *at the end of the Covenant. We are introduced to these "last" events over and over in the Old Testament with the phrases "Last Days", and "Latter Days".* Here are a few of them.

> *"And Jacob called unto his sons, and said, Gather yourselves together, that I may tell you that which shall befall you in the last days."* [Italicized] Genesis 49:1 KJV

> *"And now, behold, I go unto my people: come therefore, and I will advertise thee what this people shall do to thy people in the latter days."* [Italicized] Numbers 24:14 KJV

> *"When thou art in tribulation, and all these things are come upon thee, even in the latter days, if thou turn to the LORD thy God, and shalt be obedient unto his voice;"* [Italicized] Deuteronomy 4:30 KJV

> *"For I know that after my death ye will utterly corrupt yourselves, and turn aside from the way which I have commanded you; and evil will befall you in the latter days; because ye will do evil in the sight of the LORD, to provoke him to anger through the work of your hands."* [Italicized] Deuteronomy 31:29 KJV

> *"And it shall come to pass in the last days, that the mountain of the LORD's house shall be established in the top of the mountains, and shall be exalted above the hills; and all nations shall flow unto it."* [Italicized] Isaiah 2:2 KJV

> *"But in the last days it shall come to pass, that the mountain of the house of the Lord shall be established in the top of the mountains, and it shall be exalted above the hills; and people shall flow unto it."* [Italicized] Micah 2:4 KJV

> *"Now I am come to make thee understand what shall befall thy people in the latter days: for yet the vision is for many days."* [Italicized] Daniel 10:14 KJV

If you go back to each text and look at the surrounding passages you will find that there is no doubt that each one of these refers to the *last days of Israel and their Covenant*. So when we come to the New Testament and we begin to find these same phrases used; what should we conclude?

> *"And it shall come to pass in the last days, saith God, I will pour out of my Spirit upon all flesh: and your sons and your daughters shall prophesy, and your young men shall see visions, and your old men shall dream dreams:"* [Italicized] Acts 2:17 KJV

> *"This know also, that in the last days perilous times shall come."* [Italicized] 2 Timothy 3:1 KJV

> *"Hath in these last days spoken unto us by his Son, whom he hath appointed heir of all things, by whom also he made the worlds;"* [Italicized] Hebrews 1:2 KJV

> *"Your gold and silver is cankered; and the rust of them shall be a witness against you, and shall eat your flesh as it were fire. Ye have heaped treasure together for the last days."* [Italicized] James 5:3 KJV

> *"Knowing this first, that there shall come in the last days scoffers, walking after their own lusts,"* [Italicized] 2 Peter 3:3 KJV

> *"Little children, it is the last time: and as ye have heard that antichrist shall come, even now are there many antichrists; whereby we know that it is the last time."* [Italicized] 1 John 2:18 KJV

Can we conclude that since the Old Testament writers were writing to a Hebrew audience and about the Nation of Israel that when we come to the New Testament, the Apostles who were *all* Jewish and members of the Nation of Israel, ministering to a predominant Jewish audience would actually change the meaning and application of the terms? I do not think that is a plausible possibility.

If they were to change the meaning and application of the term Last Days, then where did they announce such a change? If they did not announce or indicate a paradigm shift in this area then why would we assume that we could insert our meaning to the phrase rather than their first century inspired meaning?

Covenant Duration

Question: When did the Old Covenant come to an end? When Jesus died on the Cross and His Blood was spilled to ratify this New Covenant. However, there was still a transition period between that time and when the Symbols of the Old were completely destroyed and the establishment of the New came fully into effect. The strength of the Old covenant was in the physical Temple and it's rituals. So it was absolutely important that these symbols were completely removed...

Covenant Duration is another vital reason why these phrases (end-times, last-days, last-times, latter-days, etc) used to describe Israel's "last days in the Old Testament" should be continued to be applied to Israel's last days in the New Testament. Apostle Paul writes:

> *"But if the ministration of death, written and engraven in stones, was glorious, so that the children of Israel could not steadfastly behold the face of Moses for the glory of his countenance; which glory was to be done away:"* [Italicized] 2 Corinthians 3:7 KJV

- Paul describes the Old Covenant as a "ministration of death", "Engraven in Stone"
- He then goes on to declare that it "—was to be done away (with)" The Old Covenant had an end.
- This end is one of the most documented and recognized ends to a country's history and existence in all of recorded history. The destruction of the Jewish Temple in AD 70 is disputed by very few as the end of the Old Covenant of Israel with God.
- Paul compares this passing Old Covenant with the New Covenant, which he says is going to remain.

> *"For if that which is done away was glorious, much more that which remaineth is glorious."* [Italicized] 2 Corinthians 3:11 KJV

All through the Old Testament, Moses and the Prophets wrote about the "Last Days" or "Latter Days" of that Old Covenant. They also prophesied that there would come a New Covenant.

> *"Behold, the days come, saith the LORD, that I will make a new covenant with the house of Israel, and with the house of Judah: 32 Not according to the covenant that I made with their fathers in the day that I took them by the hand to bring them out of the land of Egypt; which my covenant they brake, although I was an husband unto them, saith the LORD:"* [Italicized] Jeremiah 31:31-32 KJV

Other Prophets wrote about this New Covenant as well. They all agreed that this New Covenant would be an *Eternal or "Everlasting" Covenant*.

> *"Incline your ear, and come unto me: hear, and your soul shall live; and I will make an everlasting covenant with you, even the sure mercies of David."* [Italicized] Isaiah 55:3 KJV

> *"For I the LORD love judgment, I hate robbery for burnt offering; and I will direct their work in truth, and I will make an everlasting covenant with them."* [Italicized] Isaiah 61:8 KJV

> *"And I will make an everlasting covenant with them, that I will not turn away from them, to do them good; but I will put my fear in their hearts, that they shall not depart from me."* [Italicized] Jeremiah 32:40 KJV

> *"Moreover I will make a covenant of peace with them; it shall be an everlasting covenant with them: and I will place them, and multiply them, and will set my sanctuary in the midst of them for evermore."* [Italicized] Ezekiel 37:26 KJV

"But now hath he obtained a more excellent ministry, by how much also he is the mediator of a better covenant, which was established upon better promises." [Italicized and Emphasis added] Hebrews 8:6 KJV

"In that he saith, A new covenant, he hath made the first old. Now that which decayeth and waxeth old is ready to vanish away." [Italicized] Hebrews 8:13 KJV

"Now the God of peace, that brought again from the dead our Lord Jesus, that great shepherd of the sheep, through the blood of the everlasting covenant," [Italicized] Hebrews 13:20 KJV

- In reading these Passages from Hebrews we see that the author is confirming to his Jewish (Hebrew) audience that the New Covenant is "better" and established upon "Better promises".
- He re-affirms that the Old Covenant was vanishing away, meaning it had an end.
- And then he agrees with the Prophets of the Old Testament that the New Covenant established through the Blood of Jesus Christ is an "*Everlasting Covenant*".

The New (Eternal) Covenant

Let Us Consider For A Moment The Nature Of This New (Eternal) Covenant:

- In contrast to the Old Covenant it is built on better promises.
- It is a Covenant of life and not death.
- And it has no end.
- So it can be said that this New Covenant has no "Last Days".
- By definition a thing with no end would never have any last day or last days.
- So again the New Testament writers had to be writing about the end of the Old Covenant when they used the phrase "Last Days".

In addition, remember the definition of the term "Eschatology"—the study of last things. If this be the case, then how can we impose an Eschatology on a Covenant that has "No End"?

- Can the New Covenant, which has no end, actually have an Eschatology? By definition it cannot.

Paul Even Confirms This Never-Ending Nature Of The New Covenant When He Writes In Ephesians 3:21

> *"Unto him be glory in the church by Christ Jesus throughout all ages, world without end. Amen."* [Italicized] KJV

> *"To Him be glory in the church and in Christ Jesus throughout all generations forever and ever. Amen [so be it]."* [Italicized] AMP

> *"Unto him be glory in the assembly [church] in Christ Jesus to all the generations of the age of the ages. Amen."* [Italicized] YLT

The more I looked at the widely accepted view that most if not all of the New Testament is yet to be fulfilled the more I realized that there were many Scriptures that simply did not fit into the scenario of events proposed by the futurists. After much in-depth study, over the years I have come to believe that the partial fulfilled view is more true to the Scriptures.

One thing in common with the Early Church Fathers was that they all believed in an Eschatology that was indeed Victorious—Here is what some of the Early Church Fathers have said:

> Charles H. Spurgeon (1834-1892)
> I myself believe that King Jesus will reign, and the idols be utterly abolished; but I expect the same power which turned the world upside down once, will still continue to do it. The Holy Ghost would never suffer the imputation to rest upon His holy name that He was not able to convert the world. (The Life and Work of Charles Haddon Spurgeon, 1992,4:2L0)

> Jonathan Edwards (1703-1758)
> The visible kingdom of satan shall be overthrown, and the Kingdom of Christ set up on the ruins of it, everywhere throughout the whole habitable globe. (The Works of Jonathan Edwards, L974, 488)
>
> Origen of Alexandria (185-254)
> It is evident that… every form of worship will be destroyed except the religion of Christ, which will alone prevail. And indeed it will one day triumph, as its principles take possession of the minds of men more and more every day. (Origen Against Celsus, 1660, 8:68) "Celsus was a pagan philosopher of his time!"
>
> John Wesley (1703-1791)
> All unprejudiced persons may see with their eyes, that He (God) is already renewing the face of the earth: And we have strong reason to hope that the work he hath begun he will carry on unto the Day of the Lord Jesus; that he will never intermit this blessed work of his Spirit until he has fulfilled all his promises, until he hath put a period to sin and misery, and infirmity, and death; and re-established universal holiness and happiness, and caused all the inhabitants of the earth to sing together "Hallelujah." (The Works of John Wesley)

Understanding Matthew Chapter 24

In this section we will study Matthew Chapter24, a Passage that has become known as the "Olivet Discourse" because Jesus gave this teaching to His disciples while they were gathered, on the Mount of Olives. We will begin in Matthew 24:3, where the disciples asked Jesus some key questions.

> "Now as He sat on the Mount of Olives, the disciples came to Him privately, saying, "Tell us, [1] when will these things be? And [2] what *will be* the sign of Your coming, and [3] of the end of the age [world-KJV]?" [Italics and parenthesis added] NASB

In the verses that follow this one, our Lord gave answers that we will be examining. How you understand His answers determines what you believe about the end-times, the tribulation, the antichrist, and the unfolding of all future events.

After the disciples asked Jesus their questions in Matthew 24:3, Jesus answered by talking about false leaders claiming to be Christ, wars, earthquakes, famines, persecutions, and people falling away from the faith. He also talked about the Gospel being preached around the world, followed by destruction, tribulation, and people being taken away.

Christians who believe the futurist view study our Lord's answers and conclude that all of the events listed are going to happen in the future, shortly before the end of the world. I have come to a very different conclusion when studying Matthew Chapter 24. We will go through Matthew Chapter 24, verse by verse, to explain, but first we need to identify clearly the questions Jesus was asked by His Disciples.

Some translations (e.g., King James Version) end this verse with "end of the world," because the word *aion*, which is used in the original Greek, may be translated as "age" or "world." Using the term "world," futurist teachers tend to summarize the questions asked by the disciples into an inquiry about the second coming of Jesus and the end of the world. Therefore, when Jesus gives His answers in the verses that follow, all His comments are thought to be about the short period of time leading up to the end of the world. Those Teachers who believed that some of the Prophecies of the Bible have been fulfilled begin by noting that in Matthew 24:3, the disciples asked Jesus not just one question, but three questions.

Question #1: "When will these things happen?"
Question #2: "What will be THE SIGN of Your coming?"
Question #3: "What about the end of the age (world)?"

Recognizing three distinct questions dramatically changes how we understand the answers Jesus give in the verses to follow. The first question asked of Jesus was: "When will these things happen?" Before we look at Jesus' answer, we need to identify what were "*these things*" about which the disciples were asking.

Christians who have been taught the Futurist view immediately think that "*these things*" refer to the events that will precede the second coming of Jesus and the end of the world. However, we would come to a different conclusion if we truly read the context of the Passage! Matthew Chapter 23 tells us about a day when Jesus was speaking in the Temple in Jerusalem. First, He warned the crowds and His disciples to watch out for the Scribes and Pharisees.

> "Then Jesus spoke to the multitudes and to His disciples,
> 2 saying: "The scribes and the Pharisees sit in Moses' seat.
> 3 Therefore whatever they tell you to observe, *that* observe
> and do, but do not do according to their works; for they say,
> and do not do. 4 For they bind heavy burdens, hard to bear,
> and lay *them* on men's shoulders; but they *themselves* will not
> move them with one of their fingers. 5 But all their works they
> do to be seen by men. They make their phylacteries broad and
> enlarge the borders of their garments. 6 They love the best
> places at feasts, the best seats in the synagogues, 7 greetings
> in the marketplaces, and to be called by men, 'Rabbi, Rabbi.'
> 8 But you, do not be called 'Rabbi'; for One is your Teacher,
> the Christ, and you are all brethren. 9 Do not call anyone on
> earth your father; for One is your Father, He who is in heaven.
> 10 And do not be called teachers; for One is your Teacher,
> the Christ. 11 But he who is greatest among you shall be your
> servant. 12 And whoever exalts himself will be humbled, and
> he who humbles himself will be exalted." Matthew 23:1-12

He then turned directly to the religious leaders of that day. We can sense the flavour of His message to them in the first few verses of His speech—Matthew 23:13-16

> "But woe to you, scribes and Pharisees, hypocrites! For you
> shut up the kingdom of heaven against men; for you neither
> go in *yourselves,* nor do you allow those who are entering to
> go in. 14 Woe to you, scribes and Pharisees, hypocrites! For
> you devour widows' houses, and for a pretence make long
> prayers. Therefore you will receive greater condemnation. 15

> "Woe to you, scribes and Pharisees, hypocrites! For you travel land and sea to win one proselyte, and when he is won, you make him twice as much a son of hell as yourselves. 16 "Woe to you, blind guides, who say, 'Whoever swears by the temple, it is nothing; but whoever swears by the gold of the temple, he is obliged *to perform it.*'

He was rebuking the religious leaders of *that day* right in the Temple. As we read on we can pick up the intensity of His message to them! Let's look at verses 23-29:

> "Woe to you, scribes and Pharisees, hypocrites! For you pay tithe of mint and anise and cummin, and have neglected the weightier *matters* of the law: justice and mercy and faith. These you ought to have done, without leaving the others undone. 24 Blind guides, who strain out a gnat and swallow a camel! 25 "Woe to you, scribes and Pharisees, hypocrites! For you cleanse the outside of the cup and dish, but inside they are full of extortion and self-indulgence. 26 Blind Pharisee, first cleanse the inside of the cup and dish, that the outside of them may be clean also. 27 "Woe to you, scribes and Pharisees, hypocrites! For you are like whitewashed tombs, which indeed appear beautiful outwardly, but inside are full of dead *men's* bones and all uncleanness. 28 Even so you also outwardly appear righteous to men, but inside you are full of hypocrisy and lawlessness. 29 "Woe to you, scribes and Pharisees, hypocrites! Because you build the tombs of the prophets and adorn the monuments of the righteous,"

He then climaxed His stinging rebuke with some very severe judgements against the religious leaders of *that day*... Verses 33-36:

> "Serpents, brood of vipers! How can you escape the condemnation of hell? 34 Therefore, indeed, I send you prophets, wise men, and scribes: *some* of them you will kill and crucify, and *some* of them you will scourge in your synagogues and persecute from city to city, 35 that on you

> may come all the righteous blood shed on the earth, from the blood of righteous Abel to the blood of Zechariah, son of Berechiah, whom you murdered between the temple and the altar. 36 Assuredly, I say to you, all these things will come upon this [that] generation." [Parenthesis added]

As we come to the end of Matthew 23, Jesus went on to tell more specifically how *The Great Judgement* was to occur. Verses 37-38:

> "O Jerusalem, Jerusalem, the one who kills the prophets and stones those who are sent to her! How often I wanted to gather your children together, as a hen gathers her chicks under *her* wings, but you were not willing! 38 See! Your house is left to you desolate..."

The big question then is this—did these Words of Jesus come true? This we know that in order for them to be accurate they would have to come to pass around AD 70 because Jesus gave these Words around AD 30...

Typically we understand a generation to be 40 years in length (for example the Hebrew people wandered in the wilderness for 40 years until a generation passed away—Numbers 32:13; Hebrews 3:8-10!)... So if Jesus' Words were to come to pass, literally, then we should expect the judgement He declared to have fallen upon those religious leaders who were listening to His Words *at that time* and to those who were around within *their generation*!

Most, if not all Bible Scholars and Theologians agree that the New Testament Letters were written between AD 35-67, with much controversy over when the last Book was written. Some argue that the Book of Revelation was written pre AD 70 while others argue that it was written post AD 70, even as late as AD 95. What is the point to this?

Well if the Words of Jesus came to pass within the time frame He prophesied then there must be some record of it. Well if the NT was written post AD 70 then there would have been some record of it; but seeing that it was written pre-AD 70 then we have to turn to recorded history to prove its fulfilment!

Here Is What Noted Jewish Historian Flavius Josephus Wrote:

> Well history records that in AD 70 Jerusalem was completely destroyed. Within 40 years after Jesus pronounced judgement, 20,000 Roman soldiers, under the command of General Titus surrounded the city and cut off all supplies of food for four months so the people would starve. Then the soldiers came into the City and mercilessly killed more than one million Jews. They then set the Temple on fire and led away another 97,000 Jews as captives.

At that time the Jewish population was decimated. Historically, little is known about the Jews' actions or lives for the following 60 years. It was not until AD 130-135 that they began reassembling with enough strength to attempt one last rebellion against Rome. Then after three years of battling, the Romans were able to crush that rebellion killing 580,000 Jews, and Israel no more was recognized as a nation (until 1948). It also was at that time that the Roman commander ordered the Temple in Jerusalem to be demolished so completely that each and every stone was carried away and the land upon which the Temple had stood was ploughed over completely. The Temple was destroyed totally, as Jesus said it would be. (Just a point to note: Today's Western Wall, also called the Wailing Wall) in Jerusalem was never a part of the Temple that existed in Jesus' day. It was a part of the parapet (which is a wall, rampart, or elevation of earth or stone to protect soldiers) that king Herod built around the Temple area.

Here Again Is What Noted Jewish Historian Flavius Josephus Wrote:

> Josephus was a Jewish historian who lived at that time and was an eyewitness of the events. Concerning the war against and destruction of Jerusalem, Josephus wrote many things, including the following:
>
> When they (the Roman soldiers) were come to the houses to plunder them, they found in them entire families of dead men... that is of such as died by the famine; they then stood in a horror at this sight, and went out without touching anything. But although they had this commiseration for such as were

> destroyed in that manner, yet had they not the same for those that were still alive, but they ran every one through whom they met with, and obstructed the very lanes with their dead bodies, and made the whole city run with blood, to such a degree indeed that the fire of many of the houses was quenched with these men's blood. (vi:viii:5)

It is worth reading the whole of Josephus' writings about the fall of Jerusalem. What is so astounding about them is how clearly-sometimes word for word-they fulfilled the prophecy of Jesus in Matthew Chapters 23 and 24. The writings of Josephus are available in most Christian bookshops or libraries, and can be accessed freely on many websites.

Here Is What A Couple Of Early Church Fathers Said About This:

> John Wesley (1703-1791)
> This was most punctually fulfilled: for after the temple was burned, Titus, the Roman general, ordered the very foundations of it to be dug up; after which the ground on which it stood was ploughed by Turnus Rufus this generation of men now living shall not pass till all these things be done—The expression implies that a great part of that generation would be passed away, but not the whole. Just so it was; for the city and temple were destroyed thirty-nine or forty years after. (The Works of John Wesley, 1985)
>
> Eusebius (263-339)
> All this occurred in this manner in the second year of the reign of Vespasian (AD 70), according to the predictions of our Lord and Saviour Jesus Christ. (Ecclesiastical History, III:7)

The Context of Matthew Chapter 24!

Let us first of all note the context in which Matthew 24 begins. We know that in the original Greek manuscripts of the New Testament there are no Chapter breaks. Matthew 23 flows right into Matthew Chapter 24 with no interruption. Matthew 24:1-2 goes on to say:

> "Then Jesus went out and departed from the temple, and His disciples came up to show Him the buildings of the temple. 2 And Jesus said to them, "Do you not see all these things? Assuredly, I say to you, not *one* stone shall be left here upon another, that shall not be thrown down."

After repeating that the Temple would be demolished completely, Jesus walked away from the Temple with His disciples. This is where I believe that Matthew Chapter 24 should really have begun:

Then the next verse starts off saying: "Now as He sat on the Mount of Olives…"

Where is the Mount of Olives? It is the hill just outside of the Temple mount in Jerusalem. This is very important—As Jesus sat down He and His disciples were now sitting on the Mount of Olives facing the Temple, which they had just exited!

Let's place ourselves in the Disciples' shoes—what would we have asked Jesus? On the forefront of their minds was the *judgement* that Jesus just passed over Jerusalem and the Temple! So this is what they asked: *"Tell us, when will these things be (or happen)?"* In essence they were asking,—"*When will Jerusalem and the Temple be destroyed?*"

As we mentioned earlier, Futurist teachers assume that the Disciples were asking about the end of the world. However, it was not until their 3rd question that the mention of the end of the world came up.

Now Get This!

Jesus never spoke to them about the world coming to an end. He spoke to them about the Temple coming down…

- You have to remember this—to the Jews The Temple was the very centre of their *world*… So in the minds of the First Century Disciples (*all* Jews) the complete destruction of the Temple signalled the end of the world…
- So in essence they were asking if the destruction of the Temple was not going to be the end of the world, then when would that take place!!!
- So the question is *when shall these things* (referring to the destruction of the Temple and Jerusalem) *be/happen*?

As we go into the depth of Jesus' answer to this question we need to keep in mind the time frame that Jesus placed on Jerusalem and the Temple being destroyed—within a generation. He repeated the very same thing in Matthew 24:34-35 saying:

> "Assuredly, I say to you, this generation [*meaning the generation He was talking to at that time over 2000 years ago…*] will by no means pass away till all these things take place. 35 Heaven and earth will pass away, but My words will by no means pass away." [Parenthesis and italics added]

Can We Accept These Words Of Jesus Literally? Yes We Can!

We need to understand that Futurist Teachers see *all* of the events of which Jesus prophesied in Matthew 24 happening not by AD 70 but sometime in the future (and that future is running for almost 2000 years now and counting)… Therefore they *cannot* accept the time frame of *that generation*, which Jesus Christ, Himself declared in two separate Passages—Matthew 23:36 and 24:34!

Here Are A Couple Of Arguments Put Forward By The Futurist Teachers:

- The word generation used here is referring to a "race" so it means that the race of the Jewish people will not pass away before the end of the world!
- Others declare that the generation that Jesus was talking about was the generation that would see all of the "end-time" events listed in Matthew 24:4-33—that generation will not pass away until Jesus returns!

I believe that Jesus knew exactly what He was speaking about! Everything that is prophesied between Matthew 23:36 and Matthew 24:34 took place exactly as Jesus declared, during the generation that was alive when Jesus declared those words.

Here Is What Origen Of Alexandria Had To Say:

> I challenge anyone to prove my statement untrue if I say that the entire Jewish nation was destroyed less than one whole generation later on account of these sufferings, which they

inflicted on Jesus. For it was, I believe forty-two years from the time when they crucified Jesus to the destruction of Jerusalem. (Origen Against Celsus, IV:XXII)

Jesus Gave His Answer To The First Question in Matthew 24:4-28. Let Us Examine Verse-By-Verse Matthew 24:4-28!

Matthew 24:4-5 "And Jesus answered and said to them: "Take heed that no one deceives you. [5] For many will come in My name, saying, 'I am the Christ,' and will deceive many."

- Christians who have heard only the futurist view immediately place these Words of Jesus in the future, shortly before the end of the world.
- They are looking for some evil leader or several leaders to start claiming that they are the Christ.
- That is the first error we need to correct. Jesus was answering the question concerning when Jerusalem and the Temple would be destroyed.
- That event happened in AD 70, within 40 years of the time in which Jesus prophesied it. Jesus told His Disciples that soon many people would come claiming to be the Christ. For Jesus' Words to be fulfilled, those imposters would have had to come in the First Century of the Church.

Did That Happen Historically?

Yes! Right after the death of Jesus, many leaders arose capturing the hearts of the Jewish people. That may seem difficult for us to understand today, but we need to keep in mind the culture of that day. The Jewish people were desperately looking for a Messiah-someone to free them from Roman domination. Their hope and much of their religious system were based on a coming Messiah. When Jesus died, many of His followers gave up believing that He was the Messiah. Other leaders quickly arose, drawing to themselves large followings!

Here Are The Records Of Some Of The Early Church Fathers:

Eusebius of Caesarea a Roman historian. (AD 263–339)

After the Lord was taken up into heaven the demons put forth

> a number of men who claimed to be gods. (The History of the Church, 1965)
>
> The Venerable Bede (673-735—also known as Saint Bede)
> For many came forward, when destruction was hanging over Jerusalem, saying that they were Christs. (Cited in Thomas Aquinas' Golden Chain, 1956)
>
> John Wesley (1703-1791)
> And, indeed, never did so many imposters appear in the world as a few years before the destruction of Jerusalem, undoubtedly because that was the time wherein the Jews in general expected the Messiah. (The Works of John Wesley, 1985)
>
> Charles Spurgeon (1834-1892)
> A large number of imposters came forward before the destruction of Jerusalem, giving out that they were the anointed of God... (The Gospel of the Kingdom, p. 213)

Matthew 24:6-7—Wars And Rumours Of War!

> "And you will hear of wars and rumours of wars. See that you are not troubled; for all *these things* must come to pass, but the end is not yet. 7 For nation will rise against nation, and kingdom against kingdom. And there will be famines, pestilences, and earth-quakes in various places."

Approximately 2,000 years ago when Jesus was sitting on the Mount of Olives with His disciples, He prophesied of coming wars. Interestingly, there were no signs of "wars and rumours of wars" when Jesus prophesied this. The power of Rome seemed to be stable, strong, irresistible, and permanent. Historically, the period was referred to as Pax Romana, that is, "Roman Peace." Of course, the enemies of Rome would not have spoken of the time so graciously, but Rome definitely was established in that region of the world. It was at that time that Jesus prophesied of coming wars.

Did The Prophecy Of Jesus Come True Within That Generation?

Indeed! Wars began to break out all over the empire. The Jews lived in constant fear, with 50,000 Jews being slain in Seleucia and 20,000 in Caesarea. Then in AD 66, 50,000 Jews were killed in Alexandria. Within a period of 18 months, four emperors in Rome were murdered violently. Civil war broke out in the city of Rome. It was a time of great turmoil, and there were constant rumours of new rebellions.

Matthew 24:7—Famines

> "For nation will rise against nation, and kingdom against kingdom. And there will be famines, pestilences, and earthquakes in various places."

Did Famines Occur During The Generation Of The Disciples?

Let's look at Acts Chapter 11 where we are told about a *great famine*:

> "Then one of them, named Agabus, stood up and showed by the Spirit that there was going to be *a great famine throughout all the world,* which also happened in the days of Claudius Caesar. 29 Then the disciples, each according to his ability, determined to send relief to the brethren dwelling in Judea. 30 This they also did, and sent it to the elders by the hands of Barnabas and Saul." [Italics added] Acts 11:28-30

> "During this time some prophets came down from Jerusalem to Antioch. 28 One of them, named Agabus, stood up and through the Spirit predicted that *a severe famine would spread over the entire Roman world*. (This happened during the reign of Claudius.) 29 The disciples, as each one was able, decided to provide help for the brothers and sisters living in Judea. 30 This they did, sending their gift to the elders by Barnabas and Saul." [Italics added] NIV

That famine was so severe in the region of Judah that we can read two places in the New Testament where Christians took offerings to collect money for Believers suffering there (Acts 11:29-30; 1 Corinthians 16:1-20).

The Historian Josephus Wrote About The Devastation Of That Period:

> "But the famine was too hard for all other passions, and it is destructive to nothing so much as to modesty... insomuch that children pulled the very morsels that their fathers were eating out of their very mouths, and what was still more to be pitied, so did the mothers do as to their infants; and when those that were most dear were perishing under their hands, they were not ashamed to take from them the very last drops that might preserve their lives... but the seditions everywhere came upon them immediately and snatched away from them what they had gotten from others, for when they saw any house shut up, this was to them a signal that the people within had gotten some food: whereupon they broke open the doors, and ran in and took pieces of what they were eating, almost up out of their very throats, and this by force; the old men, who held their food fast, were beaten; and if the women hid what they had within their hands, their hair was torn for so doing; nor was there any commiseration shown either to the aged or to the infants, but they lifted up children from the ground as they hung upon the morsels they had gotten, and shook them down upon the floor." (v:x:3)

Knowing about this famine and the destruction of Jerusalem to follow, Jesus said to the women of Jerusalem: Luke 23:27-29

> "And a great multitude of the people followed Him, and women who also mourned and lamented Him. 28 But Jesus, turning to them, said, "Daughters of Jerusalem, do not weep for Me, but weep for yourselves and for your children. 29 For indeed the days are coming in which they will say, 'Blessed *are* the barren, wombs that never bore, and breasts which never nursed!"

Eusebius

> "Under (Claudius) the world was visited with a famine, which writers that are entire strangers to our religion have recorded in their histories." (Ecclesiastical History, II:8)

Verse 7—Earthquakes In Various Places.

Not only did the earth quake when Jesus died on the Cross (Matthew 27:51-52)! It also quaked again when He rose from the dead (Matthew 28:2). Not only then but also history tells us that the few years just prior to the fall of Jerusalem in AD 70 was a time of unusual seismic activity.

The most famous was the destruction of Pompeii (a Roman city/town) in AD63.

Several writers of the period also tell us about earthquakes at Crete, Smyrna, Miletus, Chios, Samos, Laodicea (AD 60), Hierapolis (AD 60), Campania, Colossae (AD 60), Rome and Judea (AD 65, 68, 69)...

Matthew 24:8—Birth Pangs

> "But all these things are *merely* the beginning of birth pangs." NASB

- It is common today for people trained in the futurist view to look at present-day natural disasters and claim that they are signs of the imminent return of Jesus, yet that is not what Jesus said.
- He was very clear that these signs would happen within that generation; furthermore, they would not be signs of the end of the world but "merely the beginning of birth pangs."

These birth pangs were to precede the destruction of Jerusalem and the Temple.

John Chrysostom (349-407) Archbishop of Constantinople was an important Early Church Father.

He speaks of the preludes to the troubles of the Jews. "All this is but the beginning of the birth pangs," that is, of the troubles that will befall them. (The Ancient Christian Commentary, 2002, Ib: 190)

Matthew 24:9—Persecution/Tribulation

> "Then they will deliver you to tribulation, and will kill you, and you will be hated by all nations because of My name."

The Jewish religious leaders instigated the first persecution. Saul was among those leaders who oversaw the men who were putting Christians to death. The Book of Acts describes that persecution, saying:

> "Now Saul was consenting to his death. At that time a *great persecution* arose against the church which was at Jerusalem; and they were all scattered throughout the regions of Judea and Samaria, except the Apostles." [Italics added] Acts 8:1

That "great persecution" continued to spread, and soon government officials such as King Herod got involved:

> "Now about that time Herod the king stretched out *his* hand to harass some from the church. 2 Then he killed James the brother of John with the sword. 3 And because he saw that it pleased the Jews, he proceeded further to seize Peter also." [Italics added] Acts 12:1-3

The persecution became even more intense in AD 64. That was the year when more than one third of the city of Rome burned to the ground. The significance of that event is difficult for us to grasp, on several levels.

For example if we compared it with the destruction of the Twin Towers in New York City, we would have to say that the fire in Rome was several times more devastating. At that time Rome was considered the centre of the civilized world, and more than one third of the city was destroyed.

Nero, who was the emperor at that time, blamed Christians for that terrible fire, and then he began what Church historians call "*The Great Persecution*."

The historian, Tacitus (c. AD 55-120), wrote how thousands of Christians were tortured, being covered in animal skins then torn to death by dogs, or being nailed to crosses, or being covered in tar and then lit on fire to illuminate Nero's gardens while he entertained guests in the evenings.

Matthew 24:10-13—Apostasy And False Prophets

> "And then many will be offended, will betray one another, and will hate one another. 11 Then many false prophets will rise up and deceive many. 12 And because lawlessness will abound, the love of many will grow cold. 13 But he who endures to the end shall be saved."

Soon after the death of our Lord, false prophets began appearing on the scene.

Apostle Paul warned his followers to watch out for the false prophets. One example is Apostle Paul's warning to the church at Ephesus before he departed to Rome for the final time:

> "And from Miletus he sent to Ephesus, and called the elders of the church. 18 And when they were come to him, he said unto them, Ye know, from the first day that I came into Asia, after what manner I have been with you at all seasons, 19 Serving the LORD with all humility of mind, and with many tears, and temptations, which befell me by the lying in wait of the Jews: 20 And how I kept back nothing that was profitable unto you, but have shewed you, and have taught you publicly, and from house to house, 21 Testifying both to the Jews, and also to the Greeks, repentance toward God, and faith toward our Lord Jesus Christ. 22 And now, behold, I go bound in the spirit unto Jerusalem, not knowing the things that shall befall me there: 23 Save that the Holy Ghost witnesseth in every city, saying that bonds and afflictions abide me. 24 But none of these things move me, neither count I my life dear unto myself, so that I might finish my course with joy, and the ministry, which I have received of the Lord Jesus, to testify the gospel of the grace of God. 25 And now, behold, I know that ye all, among whom I have gone preaching the kingdom of God, shall see my face no more. 26 Wherefore I take you to record this day, that I am pure from the blood of all men. 27 For I have not shunned to declare unto you all the counsel of God. 28 Take heed therefore unto yourselves, and to all the flock, over the which the Holy Ghost

> hath made you overseers, to feed the church of God, which he hath purchased with his own blood. 29 For I know this, that after my departing shall grievous wolves enter in among you, not sparing the flock. 30 Also of your own selves shall men arise, speaking perverse things, to draw away disciples after them. 31 Therefore watch, and remember, that by the space of three years I ceased not to warn every one night and day with tears. 32 And now, brethren, I commend you to God, and to the word of his grace, which is able to build you up, and to give you an inheritance among all them which are sanctified." Acts 20:17-32 KJV

Apostle John explained that during his lifetime "many false prophets have gone out into the world" 1 John 4:1-3.

> "Beloved, believe not every spirit, but try the spirits whether they are of God: because many false prophets are gone out into the world. 2 Hereby know ye the Spirit of God: Every spirit that confesseth that Jesus Christ is come in the flesh is of God: 3 And every spirit that confesseth not that Jesus Christ is come in the flesh is not of God: and this is that spirit of antichrist, whereof ye have heard that it should come; and even now already is it in the world." KJV

Similarly, Apostle Peter warned, false prophets and false teachers.

> "But there were false prophets also among the people, even as there shall be false teachers among you, who privily shall bring in damnable heresies, even denying the Lord that bought them, and bring upon themselves swift destruction. 2 And many shall follow their pernicious ways; by reason of whom the way of truth shall be evil spoken of. 3 And through covetousness shall they with feigned words make merchandise of you: whose judgment now of a long time lingereth not, and their damnation slumbereth not. 4 For if God spared not the angels that sinned, but cast them down to hell, and delivered them into chains of darkness, to be reserved unto judgment; 5 And

spared not the old world, but saved Noah the eighth person, a preacher of righteousness, bringing in the flood upon the world of the ungodly;" 2 Peter 2:1-5 KJV

The first major group was the Judaizers, who taught that Gentiles had to become Jewish proselytes and adhere to the Law of Moses as well as have faith in Christ. Then came the Gnostics. They arose as soon as Christians brought the gospel to Greek-minded people, and by the year AD 150, about one third of all Christians were involved in Gnosticism. To grasp the influence of this heresy, imagine how it would be today if one third of all Christians in your own community were taken in by a certain heretical teaching. That is exactly what happened during those early days when the Church was struggling to survive.

Since our understanding of Gnosticism is key to understanding the problems of the First and Second Century Church. Let us briefly explore the meaning and teachings of this cult/group.

Gnosticism:

The name is derived from the Greek word "*gnosis*" which literally means "*knowledge.*"

- At the foundation of First-Century Gnosticism was a worldview in which the spiritual world was distinctly separated from the natural world.
- The spiritual world was considered good, and the natural world was considered corrupt.
- The leaders of this teaching/belief concluded that God could not have taken on flesh or come into this corrupt world in the form of Jesus. This led to several false teachings about the nature of Jesus.
- Thinking of this natural world as corrupt also led them to believe that a person must be very spirit-conscious to be a good Christian. Hence, they developed mystical understandings and taught that a person must have secret knowledge to know God. From this the word Gnosticism came, for it literally means "knowledge."
- During the first century, Gnosticism took many forms, but one of the most influential Gnostic groups completely rejected the Old

Testament. They declared that the God of the Old Testament was the devil and Jesus had come to reveal an "unknown Father" to us.

- Other Gnostics taught that the Old Testament rituals were still valid for Christians.
- One of the most prominent Gnostic teachers was a man called Cerinthus. He was a Jew who lived in Asia Minor, teaching that Jesus was the son of Joseph and Mary (not born of a virgin)—an ordinary man. A heavenly spirit called "the Christ" came upon Jesus at His baptism and left Him at the crucifixion. Jesus had brought secret teachings that would enable people to overcome enslavement to the physical world, but the Jewish customs also had to be observed. Those who proved faithful to these teachings and observances would live for a literal 1,000 years of sensual pleasures. These teachings of Cerinthus flourished throughout Asia Minor.
- Historical records tell us that he Apostle John was so horrified at Cerinthus' teachings that on one occasion when John walked into the public baths with his disciples at Ephesus, he saw Cerinthus and ran out of the bathhouse, warning his disciples that the house may fall down because "Cerinthus, the enemy of the truth, is inside."
- This is the setting in which Apostle John ministered. History tells us that by the year AD 150, one third of all Christians were under the influence of Gnosticism. It was a huge cult and a major concern of the Church fathers. John was on the front lines of that battle.

Apostle John wrote to correct Gnostic teachings. As soon as we learn about the historical setting in which he ministered, we can more easily understand his writings.

- For example, his Gospel starts off saying: In the beginning was the Word, and the Word was with God, and the Word was God... And the Word became flesh, and dwelt among us, and we saw His glory. (John 1:1-14)
- Do you see how profound this statement is? Because the Gnostics thought of the natural world as evil, they could not

believe that Jesus could have been God and at the same time have taken on human flesh. John boldly told the reader that he saw Jesus. Jesus was real. Jesus came into this world. John declared that Jesus is God and Jesus took on flesh.

- John was also countering Gnosticism when he wrote his first Two Epistles. First John starts with a declaration that is diametrically opposed to the Gnostic view of Jesus.

> "What was from the beginning, what we have heard, what we have seen with our eyes, what we have looked at and touched with our hands, concerning the Word of Life—2 and the life was manifested, and we have seen and testify and proclaim to you the eternal life, which was with the Father and was manifested to us." 1 John 1:1-2 NASB

Do you see how clearly and forcefully John is confronting Gnosticism? John said that he and the other Apostles heard Jesus, saw Him, and touched Him with their hands. Jesus manifested Himself in this world. He was God, and He took on flesh. This battle that John had with Gnosticism is common knowledge among Bible scholars. In fact, any student serious about understanding John's writings will be ever conscious of this fact.

Matthew 24:14—Preaching the Gospel

What about Matthew 24:14? "This gospel of the kingdom shall be preached in the whole world as a testimony to all the nations, and then the end will come."

If you have been trained under the futurist view, you know that this verse is often quoted to encourage Christians to help get the gospel spread around the world so that Jesus Christ can return. And *YES* we must preach the Gospel of The Kingdom, *UNTIL* Jesus Returns…
However: Let Us Look At Another Way To Understand This Scripture.

- Jesus said that all of the events of which He spoke would happen in that generation. If we are going to believe the Words of Jesus literally, then we must look to see how this Verse could have been fulfilled in the First Century.

Letting The Bible Interpret Itself:

Any serious study of Scripture must apply the foundational principles of biblical study, one being that other Bible passages that talk about the same topics should be read before drawing any conclusions about what a specific passage means. In this way, we allow the Bible to interpret itself, with fewer misunderstandings due to our own biases and cultural influences. For example, for us to understand Matthew 24:14, it will be helpful to find out if there are other Bible passages that talk about the gospel being preached to the whole world. If you do this in your own study, you will discover five passages that address this subject. Amazingly, all five passages reveal to us how the gospel was proclaimed to all nations within the generation of the Apostles. Let's look at those five passages.

- First, examine the words of Apostle Paul in Romans 1:8: First, I thank my God through Jesus Christ for you all, because your faith is being proclaimed throughout the whole world.
- Their faith is being proclaimed—in Paul's lifetime— throughout the whole world.
- Apostle Paul makes this even clearer in Romans 10:18:

"But I say, surely they have never heard, have they? Indeed they have; "Their voice has gone out into all the earth, and their words to the ends of the world." NASB

- Apostle Paul says this again in Romans 16:25-26:

"Now to Him who is able to establish you according to my gospel and the preaching of Jesus Christ, according to the revelation of the mystery which has been kept secret for long ages past, 26 but now is manifested, and by the Scriptures of the prophets, according to the commandment of the eternal God, has been made known to all the nations, *leading* to obedience of faith…" NASB

"According to my (Apostle Paul's message) gospel and the preaching of Jesus Christ…" has been made known to all the nations (in Apostle Paul's time, over 2000 years ago).

• Apostle Paul tells us this again in Colossians 1:5-6:

> "Because of the hope laid up for you in heaven, of which you previously heard in the word of truth, the gospel 6 which has come to you, just as in all the world also it is constantly bearing fruit and increasing, even as *it has been doing* in you also since the day you heard *of it* and understood the grace of God in truth;" NASB

The Gospel, which has come to you, just as in all the world also it, is constantly bearing fruit and increasing. There it is again. The gospel was bearing fruit in all the world—in Paul's lifetime.

• Finally, Let's Look At The Clearest Statement Paul Made On This Subject: Colossians 1:23

> "If indeed you continue in the faith firmly established and steadfast, and not moved away from the hope of the gospel that you have heard, which was proclaimed in all creation under heaven, and of which I, Paul, was made a minister." NASB

Could Paul have stated it any clearer? The Gospel was proclaimed "in all creation under heaven."

As folks read these passages they may wonder if the words "whole world," "ends of the world," "all the world," and "all creation under heaven," really mean the whole world in the way we understand today. Some may question if these words perhaps meant the world as far as the Disciples knew it or just the Roman Empire.

In these Passages there are two different Greek words that have been translated into the word "world." Paul used the Greek word kosmos in Romans 1:8 and in Colossians 1:6. The word kosmos can be translated as "world" or "earth," but either way, it includes the entire world.

The other Greek word for world is oikoumene, which can be translated "inhabited earth" or "civilized earth." Paul used this word in Romans 10:18, when he declared that the Word had gone out "to the ends of the world." Jesus also used this word, oikoumene, in Matthew

24:14. Hence, we understand that His original declaration was that the Disciples would have time to preach the gospel of the Kingdom to the then civilized world. However we look at it, the Words of Jesus were fulfilled within the generation of the First Disciples. They did turn the world upside down.

- John Chrysostom: You will preach everywhere… Then he added, "This gospel of the kingdom will be preached throughout the whole world, as a testimony to all nations; and the end will come." The sign of this final end time will be the downfall of Jerusalem. (The Ancient Christian Commentary, 2002, Ib: 191)
- Justin Martyr: From Jerusalem there went out into the world, men, twelve in number… by the power of God they proclaimed to every race of men that they were sent by Christ to teach to all the word of God. (The Ante-Nicene Fathers, 1989, First Apology, XXXIX)
- Eusebius: The teaching of the New Covenant was borne to all nations, and at once the Romans besieged Jerusalem and destroyed it and the Temple. (The Proof of the Gospel, I:VI)
- Charles Spurgeon: There was a sufficient interval for the full proclamation of the gospel by the Apostles and Evangelists of the early Christian Church, and for the gathering out of those who recognized the crucified Christ as the true Messiah. Then came the awful end, which the Saviour foresaw and foretold, and the prospect of which wrung from his lips and heart the sorrowful lament that followed his prophecy of the doom awaiting his guilty capital. (Spurgeon's Popular Exposition of Matthew, 1979, p. 211)

After they preached the gospel successfully, Jesus said, "and then the end will come" [Matthew 24:14].

What End Was He Referring To?

Remember, He was answering their question, "When will Jerusalem and the Temple be destroyed?" That is the "*End*" about which Jesus was speaking. Indeed, that destruction is what Jesus talked about next.

The Temple of God—His Dwelling Place

Please remember this: God's first interaction with mankind began in the Garden where He would come and have Fellowship with Adam and Eve in the cool of the day. After they sinned and God raised up a People to Himself (the Jews), He instructed Moses to pitch a Tent in which He would come and interact with them…

King Solomon built the first permanent Temple in 957 BC on direct orders from God. And it replaced the Tent… The dimensions were very specific and we all knew what occurred when the first Temple was dedicated… God's Glory came down and filled it.

During the ensuing years many attempts were made by the heathen nations to destroy it; but they were all unsuccessful until 586 BC when it was completely destroyed by the Babylonians when they sacked the City…

According to the Book of Ezra, work on building (rebuilding) the Second Temple began in 538 BC, which was authorized by King Cyrus, the Great under the direct orders from God. God called King Cyrus His Anointed! It was completed 23 years later and was dedicated in 515 BC.

Several attempts were made to destroy it after being rebuilt and dedicated in 515 BC but they were all unsuccessful. It was not until AD 70 that the Temple was completely destroyed, fulfilling the Prophecy of Jesus the Messiah; that Not One Stone was going to be left on top one another.

There was never any mandate given by God for it to be rebuilt. As a matter of fact Jesus Christ had already begun to declare that His Father's true intent was never for Him to dwell in Temples made with men hands. Or that He never intended for Worship to Him to be done from a "Specific, Physical Holy Place" as was revealed through His conversation with the Woman at The Well:

> "The woman said to Him, "Sir, I perceive that You are a prophet. 20 Our fathers worshiped on this mountain, and you *Jews* say that in Jerusalem is the place where one ought to worship." 21 Jesus said to her, "Woman, believe Me, the hour is coming when you will neither on this mountain, nor in Jerusalem, worship the Father. 22 You worship what you do not know;

we know what we worship, for salvation is of the Jews. 23 But the hour is coming, and now is, when the true worshipers will worship the Father in spirit and truth; for the Father is seeking such to worship Him. 24 God *is* Spirit, and those who worship Him must worship in spirit and truth." 25 The woman said to Him, "I know that Messiah is coming" [who is called Christ]. "When He comes, He will tell us all things." 26 Jesus said to her, "I who speak to you am *He.*" John 4:19-26 NASB

"Our fathers had the tabernacle of witness in the wilderness, as He appointed, instructing Moses to make it according to the pattern that he had seen, 45 which our fathers, having received it in turn, also brought with Joshua into the land possessed by the Gentiles, whom God drove out before the face of our fathers until the days of David, 46 who found favour before God and asked to find a dwelling for the God of Jacob. 47 But Solomon built Him a house. 48 "However, the Most High does not dwell in temples made with hands, as the prophet says: 49 *'Heaven is My throne, And earth is My footstool. What house will you build for Me? says the LORD, Or what is the place of My rest? 50 Has My hand not made all these things?*" [Italics added] Acts 7:44-50 NASB

"Now while Paul waited for them at Athens, his spirit was provoked within him when he saw that the city was given over to idols. 17 Therefore he reasoned in the synagogue with the Jews and with the *Gentile* worshipers, and in the marketplace daily with those who happened to be there. 18 Then certain Epicurean and Stoic philosophers encountered him. And some said, "What does this babbler want to say?" Others said, "He seems to be a proclaimer of foreign gods," because he preached to them Jesus and the resurrection. 19 And they took him and brought him to the Areopagus, saying, "May we know what this new doctrine *is* of which you speak? 20 For you are bringing some strange things to our ears. Therefore we want to know what these things mean." 21 For all the Athenians and the foreigners who were there spent their time in nothing else

> but either to tell or to hear some new thing. 22 Then Paul stood in the midst of the Areopagus and said, "Men of Athens, I perceive that in all things you are very religious; 23 for as I was passing through and considering the objects of your worship, I even found an altar with this inscription: TO THE UNKNOWN GOD. Therefore, the One whom you worship without knowing, Him I proclaim to you: 24 God, who made the world and everything in it, since He is Lord of heaven and earth, does not dwell in temples made with hands. 25 Nor is He worshiped with men's hands, as though He needed anything, since He gives to all life, breath, and all things."
> Acts 17:16-25 NASB

So no matter what popular opinion says—God did not and has not authorized any rebuilding of the Jewish temple. And if for any reason one is rebuilt God will not be taking up residence there...

Matthew 24:15-20—Warning of Destruction

Jesus told the Disciples that after they successfully preached the gospel in every nation or in the then inhabited earth; they needed to be ready to flee from Judea, because destruction was about to occur.

> "Therefore when you see the 'abomination of desolation, spoken of by Daniel the prophet, standing in the holy place" [whoever reads, let him understand], 16 "then let those who are in Judea flee to the mountains. 17 Let him who is on the housetop not go down to take anything out of his house. 18 And let him who is in the field not go back to get his clothes. 19 But woe to those who are pregnant and to those who are nursing babies in those days! 20 And pray that your flight may not be in winter or on the Sabbath." NASB

Christians trained in the futurist view envision this passage being fulfilled in the future, before the end of the world. Typically, they think of the abomination of desolation as the antichrist who will walk into the Temple (one that they declare, will be built in the near future) in Jerusalem, set up an idol of himself, and declare himself as God. That event is thought to begin a terrible worldwide tribulation.

- To understand this passage please note that Jesus is talking about tragic events that will happen not throughout the world, but right there in Jerusalem and the surrounding area of Judea.
- We know this because He is talking to His Disciples and answering their question about when Jerusalem and the Temple will be destroyed.
- Jesus said that when the abomination of desolation (which will be defined later in this chapter) stands in the Holy Place, people "*in Judea*" are to run to the mountains.
- *He did not say that people all over the world should flee.*
- Further, we know that Jesus was addressing His warning to the Jews, for He warned people to pray that their flight may not be on the Sabbath—a warning that is particularly relevant to Jewish people, as they kept the Sabbath in a fashion that did not allow them to work or run—even in the event of a tragedy.
- Also, He said that people on their housetops must not go into their houses to get their possessions; that too indicates that He was talking about people in that region of the world, for houses in Jerusalem often were constructed in a way in which people could gather on their rooftops.
- Jesus' warning tells us nothing about people living outside of Judea.
- Jesus was speaking of something terrible about to happen in Judea, and there is nothing in the passage to indicate a worldwide event.

The Parallel Passages Are in Mark Chapter 13; Luke Chapter 21

To confirm that Jesus was speaking in Matthew 24:15-20 of events to happen around Jerusalem and Judea, it is helpful to glance at the Gospels of Mark and Luke where the Olivet Discourse is also recorded. In looking at these parallel passages, it is worth noting how closely they correspond with Matthew Chapter 24.

- Jesus exposed the wickedness of the Jewish religious leaders, and pronounced condemnation and judgement upon them... (Matthew 23:1-35; Mark 12:38-40; Luke 20:45-47).
- Jesus declared the Temple's destruction (Matthew 23:37-24:2; Mark 13:1-2 Luke 21:5-6)
- The Disciples questioned Jesus about the coming destruction (Matthew 24:3; Mark 13:3-4; Luke 21:7).

- Jesus answered, talking about:
- People claiming to be Christ (Matthew 24:5; Mark 13:5-6; Luke 21:8)!
- Wars and rumours of war (Matthew 24:6-7; Mark 13:7-8; Luke 21:9-10)!
- Earthquakes and famines (Matthew 24:7; Mark 13:8; Luke 21:11)!
- And the Gospel being preached all over the then world (Matthew 24:14; Mark 13:10)!

These passages are amazingly similar, although each writer used slightly different terminology. After Jesus talked about the signs that would take place, He went on in each Gospel to warn that people would have to flee from Judea.

Let's Examine The Accounts In The Three Parallel Passages.

> *"Therefore when you see the 'abomination of desolation, spoken of by Daniel the prophet, standing in the holy place" [whoever reads, let him understand], 16 "then let those who are in Judea flee to the mountains."* [Italicized] Matthew 24:15-16 KJV

> *"But when you see Jerusalem surrounded by armies, then recognize that her desolation is near. Then those who are in Judea must flee to the mountains."* [Italicized] Luke 21:20-21 KJV

> *"But when you see the abomination of desolation standing where it should not be [let the reader understand], then those who are in Judea must flee to the mountains."* [Italicized] Mark 13:14 KJV

Notice that in all three passages Jesus clearly states that it is the people in Judea who are to flee. Nowhere in any of the passages does He speak of or refer to any broader region.

The Abomination In The Holy Place:

Now we need to examine what Jesus was referring to when He warned the Disciples about an abomination of desolation standing in the holy place.

- As mentioned earlier, futurist teachers assume that the abomination is the antichrist who will setup an idol in a future temple or actually step into that temple and declare himself as God.
- To see how unfounded that understanding is, first note that the antichrist is never mentioned in Matthew Chapter 24 (nor in any of the Gospels).
- Also, note that Jesus was talking to His Disciples and telling them that they will witness this event.
- Jesus was not talking about an antichrist who would come hundreds or even thousands of years later, but rather some abomination that would be seen in their lifetime.

Next, we can identify where the abomination was to stand. Matthew refers to the "Holy Place" and Luke refers to "Jerusalem." Which author is correct? Both.

- When Matthew mentions the Holy Place, he was referring to the same location as Luke when he referred to Jerusalem.
- We can confirm this by examining the terminology "holy place," which has been translated from the Greek words hagios topos. This terminology is never used anywhere in the Bible to refer to the Temple or the holy of holies in the Temple (where futurist teachers declare the antichrist will sit).
- As anyone with a Greek dictionary can learn the word hagios means holy and the word topos refers to a locality. It is used in expressions such as a "desert place" but never in reference to a building.
- Since we have Luke referring to this holy place as "Jerusalem," it follows that Jesus was referring to Jerusalem in the parallel passage of Matthew.

Next, what is the abomination of desolation? When we speak of an abomination, we are referring to a horrible, detestable, disgusting thing. Luke tells us that the abomination was the armies surrounding Jerusalem. What could be more detestable to Jewish people?

"But when you see Jerusalem surrounded by armies, then recognize that her desolation is near. 21 Then those who are in

> *Judea must flee to the mountains.*" [Italicized] Luke 21:20-21 KJV

The Heathen Armies Would Gather To Make The Holy City A Desolation.
Does this correspond with historical evidence? Perfectly!

- As we have noted, in the year AD 70, 20,000 Roman soldiers lined the mountains around Jerusalem, surrounding the holy city.
- John Chrysostom (349-407)... the abomination of desolation means the army by which the holy city of Jerusalem was made desolate. (The Ante-Nicene Fathers)

This description also matches the one we read in Daniel 9. Remember that Jesus referred in Matthew 24:15 to the abomination of desolation "about which Daniel spoke." Note Daniel's reference to the abomination:

> "The people of the prince who is to come will destroy the city and the sanctuary. And its end will come with a flood; even to the end there will be war; desolations are determined." Daniel 9:26 KJV

Indeed, the soldiers came to destroy Jerusalem. For four months they starved the people; then they descended upon the city as a flood pouring into the valley. Fleeing Jerusalem and Judea when the abomination—that is, the Roman soldiers—began lining the mountains around Jerusalem, there was a short time during which people could flee. Hence, we can understand our Lord's exhortation for those on the housetops not to go down to get their possessions, nor those in the field to return to get their cloaks. Jesus was telling them that they must flee immediately.

After those Christians in Jerusalem were allowed to escape, the Roman soldiers sealed off the city. No one else was allowed to go in or out. The Romans cut Jerusalem off so the people would starve.

> Josephus wrote: So all hope of escaping was now cut off from the Jews, together with their liberty of going out of the city. Then did the famine widen its progress, and devoured

> the people by whole houses and families; the upper rooms were full of women and children that were dying by famine; and the lanes of the city were full of the dead bodies of the aged; the children also and the young men wandered about the marketplaces like shadows, all swelled with the famine, and fell down dead, wheresoever their misery seized them. (The Wars of the Jews, 1998, v:xii:3)

Historically, we know that the early Disciples fled Jerusalem before the destruction of the city. Why did they flee? Because they remembered the warning that Jesus gave them, that the city would be surrounded by armies and they must flee to escape the devastation to follow.

> Eusebius: The members of the Jerusalem church, by means of an oracle given by revelation to acceptable persons there, were ordered to leave the City before the war began and settle in a town in Peraea called Pella. (The History of the Church, 1965, III:5)

> The Venerable Bede: When on the approach of the war with Rome and the extermination of the Jewish people, all the Christians who were in that province, warned by the prophecy, fled far away, as Church history relates, and retiring beyond Jordan, remained for a time in the city of Pella. (Cited in Thomas Aquinas' Golden Chain, Dec. 1, 07,)

> Charles Spurgeon: The Christians in Jerusalem and the surrounding towns and villages, "in Judea", availed themselves of the first opportunity for eluding the Roman armies, and fled to the mountain city of Pella, in Perea, where they were preserved from the general destruction which overthrew the Jews. There was no time to spare before the final investment of the guilty city; the man "on the house-top" could "not come down to take anything out of his house", and the man "in the field" could not "return back, to take his clothes." They must flee to the mountains in the greatest haste the moment that

> they saw "Jerusalem compassed with armies." (The Gospel of the Kingdom, 1974, p. 215)
>
> John Chrysostom: "Then let those who are in Judea flee to the mountains." When does he mean by "then"? These things will take place, he says, "when you see the desolating sacrilege spoken of by the prophet Daniel, standing in the holy place." He seems to me to be speaking of the armies and wars. So flee. There is no hope of safety for you in the cities. (The Ancient Christian Commentary, 2002, Ib: 193)

Matthew 24:21-22—A Great Tribulation

Jesus warned the Disciples to flee from Judea (Matthew 24:15-20). Then He prophesied the great destruction to follow:

> "For then there will be *a great tribulation*, such as has not occurred since the beginning of the world until now, nor ever will. 22 Unless those days had been cut short, no life would have been saved; but for the sake of the elect those days will be cut short." [Italics added] Matthew 24:21-22 NASB

Futurist teachers say that this great tribulation will come in the future, just before the end of the world, and it will spread over all the earth. This coming tribulation is talked about so much in some Christian circles that it has developed its own identity and is called "The Great Tribulation." In reality, Jesus was talking about the destruction of Jerusalem in AD 70. He was answering the Disciples' question, "When will Jerusalem and the Temple be destroyed?"

If Jesus truly was talking about the events of AD 70, then we have another question to answer. How could He have said that nothing so terrible has occurred since the beginning of the world until now, nor ever will?

- Haven't there been more wicked things happen than the destruction of Jerusalem?
- What about the twentieth-century Holocaust when 6 million Jews were murdered?
- What about other times of war and mass destruction?

- The destruction of Jerusalem was not the greatest in magnitude, but Jesus was talking in terms of it being the greatest calamity in the sense of suffering and anguish.

Josephus Describes For Us What Actually Took Place In AD 70. After the city was sealed off by the Roman soldiers, Josephus tells how the Jews committed terrible atrocities to each other, even horrific actions, such as cannibalism, which occurred during the famine. He narrates a vile account of a woman murdering her small son, cooking him, and eating half of him, then arguing with thieves, who broke into her house looking for food, as to who would eat the other half. During the famine, Jews also swallowed diamonds and precious stones in hopes of escaping and safely carrying them to new locations. Knowing this, the Roman soldiers would capture individuals from the city and cut open their stomachs and entrails, searching for whatever they could find. After General Titus put an end to those searchings, a new form of torture began. Josephus wrote that as men tried to escape the city or to crawl out to gather food, the Roman soldiers would cut off their hands and send them back inside the city. When the Roman soldiers finally were given the order to descend upon Jerusalem, Josephus tells us that more than 500 men were caught per day, then whipped, tortured, and crucified. Men were nailed to crosses in front of the city until there was no more space. Finally, the soldiers entered the city, and every person was killed except for 97,000, who were taken away to be slaves in the Egyptian mines or as gifts to various provinces so that they might be killed in the theatres.[7] When Jerusalem was destroyed, a genocide of Jews was triggered throughout the surrounding regions. Josephus said: There was not any one Syrian city, which did not slay their Jewish inhabitants, and were not more bitter enemies to us than were the Romans themselves. (The Wars of the Jews, 1998, vii:viii:7)

History provides many similar reports of what took place throughout the whole of the Roman Empire. When we compare the genocide of AD 70 to the Jewish Holocaust of the twentieth century, we must admit that the more recent Holocaust was greater in number, with 6 million Jews killed over a six-year period. Living in labour camps and being killing with poisonous gas was horrific, but as far as we know, no one was crucified. In AD 70 more than one million Jews were starved, tortured and killed in a four-month period. Despite the twentieth century Holocaust's larger magnitude, the violence during the AD 70 tribulation ended the lives of a much greater percentage of the Jewish population and was far more extreme in the atrocities that were committed.

> Charles Spurgeon: The destruction of Jerusalem was more terrible than anything that the world has ever witnessed, either before or since. Even Titus seemed to see in his cruel work the hand of an avenging God. Truly, the blood of the martyrs slain in Jerusalem was amply avenged when the whole city became a veritable Aceldama, or field of blood. (Spurgeon's Popular Exposition of Matthew, 1979, p. 211)

> Eusebius: Thousands and thousands of men of every age who together with women and children perished by the sword, by starvation, and by countless other forms of death... all this anyone who wishes can gather in precise detail from the pages of Josephus's history. I must draw particular attention to his statement that the people who flocked together from all Judaea at the time of the Passover Feast and—to use his own words—were shut up in Jerusalem as if in a prison, totalled nearly three million. (The History of the Church, 1965, p. 69)

Matthew 24:23-27—False Christs Appear

As people were being slaughtered throughout Judea, many Jews held to their hopes of a Messiah appearing to deliver them at the last moment. Several leaders took advantage of this belief, which was so fundamental to the Jewish heart and mind.

Knowing that this would happen, Jesus gave a warning:

> "Then if anyone says to you, 'Behold, here is the Christ,' or 'There He is,' do not believe him. 24 For false christs and false prophets will arise and will show great signs and wonders, so

> as to mislead, if possible, even the elect. 25 Behold, I have told you in advance. 26 So if they say to you, 'Behold, He is in the wilderness,' do not go out, or 'Behold, He is in the inner rooms,' do not believe them. 27 For just as the lightning comes from the east and flashes even to the west, so will the coming of the Son of Man be." Matthew 24:23-27 NASB

Josephus Wrote Of Many False Prophets And Leaders Claiming To Be The Christ.

One example he gave was of a false prophet who publicly declared to the desperate Jerusalem dwellers, that on a certain day, God was going to supernaturally deliver them. Many Jews followed that leader and ended up losing their lives because of their false hope. Josephus also described how extraordinary signs appeared, including a star resembling a sword over Jerusalem and then a light around the Temple for a half hour. (The War of The Jews)

Just As Jesus Had Prophesied, the false christs Demonstrated "Great Signs And Wonders."

Saint Jerome: (347-420) At the time of the Jewish captivity by Rome, many Jewish elders claimed to be the Christ. There were so many, in fact, that there were three distinct camps of them when the Romans besieged Jerusalem. (The Ancient Christian Commentary, 2002, Ib: 197)

Jesus warned the Disciples not to listen to any rumours or declarations of false christs or false prophets appearing. Then He made a declaration contrasting the false to the real. He said: "For just as the lightning comes from the east and flashes even to the west, so will the coming of the Son of Man be." (Matthew 24:23-27) from this they were to know that Jesus' coming would not happen in the wilderness or in some secret place. When the Messiah truly came, Jesus said, it would happen up above.

The Corpse and Vultures

Matthew 24:28: "Wherever the corpse is, there the vultures will gather." Envision thousands of soldiers gathered on the mountains encircling Jerusalem. Now add to that picture the banner under which they assembled—the banner of the vulture, which Roman soldiers carried on flags and often painted on their shields. As a Prophet,

Jesus declared that the vultures would gather, and Jerusalem would be the corpse.

Confirmation From the Parallel Gospels

Jesus finished answering the first question, having explained all of the signs that would lead up to the destruction of Jerusalem and the Temple.

Before we go on to examine His answer to the second question, it is worth pointing out the confirmation of two other Gospels. We discussed how closely Mark Chapter 13 and Luke Chapter 21 parallel Matthew Chapter 24. There is, however, one key difference. In Matthew 24:3 the disciples asked Jesus three questions:

- Question #1: "When will these things happen?"
- Question #2: "What will be the sign of Your coming?"
- Question #3: "What about the end of the age (world)?"

In contrast, neither Mark nor Luke records the second or third questions. Luke 21:5-7 goes like this:

> "And while some were talking about the temple, that it was adorned with beautiful stones and votive gifts, He said, 6 "As for these things which you are looking at, the days will come in which there will not be left one stone upon another which will not be torn down." 7 They questioned Him, saying, "Teacher, when therefore will these things happen? And what will be the sign when these things are about to take place?" NASB

Mark 13:1-4 reads very similarly to this passage, without asking anything about the signs of our Lord's coming or of the end of the world.

> "As He was going out of the temple, one of His disciples said to Him, "Teacher, behold what wonderful stones and what wonderful buildings!" 2 And Jesus said to him, "Do you see these great buildings? Not one stone will be left upon another which will not be torn down." 3 As He was sitting on the Mount of Olives opposite the temple, Peter and James and John and Andrew were questioning Him privately, 4 "Tell us, when will

these things be, and what *will be* the sign when all these things are going to be fulfilled?" NASB

This is significant because it gives us a clear framework in which to understand Matthew Chapter 24. Since Mark and Luke record only the question about when the Temple would be destroyed, we know that our Lord was answering that question when He talked about people claiming to be Christ, wars, earthquakes, famines, persecutions, etc.

The answers Jesus gave in Mark and Luke are almost identical to the answers He gave in Matthew 24:4-22. Therefore, it is only reasonable to conclude that Jesus was talking about the Temple's destruction when He talked about people claiming to be Christ, wars, earthquakes, famines, persecutions, etc. This is confirmation that Matthew 24:4-22 is answering the first question only.

Acknowledging the parallels in the Gospels shows again how wrong futurist teachers are when they try to combine all three questions recorded in Matthew 24:3, as if they all are asking about the Second Coming and the end of the world.

We will look at the answers Jesus gave to the two remaining questions, and, indeed, we will talk about His coming and the end of the world, because those are the second and third questions. However, make no mistake that the first question was about the destruction of Jerusalem and the Temple. That happened in AD 70, within the generation of the disciples, exactly as Jesus prophesied.

Closing The First Question—A Few Points To Note:

We cannot emphasize enough how significant an event it was when Jerusalem and the Temple were destroyed.

- Jerusalem was the "Holy City."
- Mount Moriah, upon which the Temple stood, was the site where Abraham was willing to offer his son Isaac—Genesis 22:2.
- It was also the place where God appeared to David—2 Chronicles 3:1.
- It was the site upon which Solomon had built the first Temple. It was there that the High Priests offered sacrifices for the sins of the people.

- It was the centre of Jewish life, a deeply sacred site.
- When the Temple was destroyed, the Jewish heritage was destroyed. In one sense, they were cut off from God. They lost their identity. Their religious system was abolished.

Remember that the writer of Hebrews explained how the Jewish religious system was abolished and replaced with the New Covenant established through Jesus. When He said: "A new covenant," He has made the first obsolete. But whatever is becoming obsolete and growing old is ready to disappear." Hebrews 8:13

- We have a New Covenant with better promises.
- We have a High Priest (Jesus Christ) who has made the ultimate and final sacrifice.
- The transition from the Old to the New stands at the centre of history and the Bible.
- It is a pivotal point in God's plan through the ages.
- When the Temple in Jerusalem was destroyed, it finalized the end of the old religious system.

Question #2: "What Will Be The Sign Of Your Coming?"

We have already explained how all of the signs, such as wars, earthquakes, famines, etc., were signs preceding the destruction of the Temple in AD 70. Those signs were fulfilled. They are not for our future.

Now we need to determine what the Disciples meant when they asked, "What will be the sign of Your coming?" When people read that question today, they have a very different mind-set than the Disciples had 2,000 years ago.

When the Disciples were sitting with Jesus on the Mount of Olives, they were not thinking about the Second Coming of our Lord. In fact, at that time in their lives they were not convinced that Jesus was going to die (Matthew 16:21-23), let alone return to earth someday. Therefore, they could not have been asking about the Second Coming. What, then, were they asking? Look again at the question:

"What will be the sign of Your coming?"

What is meant by His "coming?"—At that time in history, the Jews were looking for a Messiah; that was their primary hope. They were looking for a Messiah to come and set up a kingdom in which the Jews would have dominion over the whole earth and reign forever.

Knowing this gives us an entirely different outlook on the thinking of the Disciples. Remember when the mother of the sons of Zebedee asked Jesus if her two sons could sit, one on His right and the other on His left (Matthew 20:20-23)? That reveals what was on their minds. When the Disciples asked Jesus, "What will be the sign of Your coming?" they were asking Him, "When will You come into Your kingdom?" "When will You take Your position and reveal Yourself as king?"

When did that happen?

After Jesus died, rose from the dead, and ascended into Heaven, He sat down on a throne at the right hand of God. All authority was given to Him, both in Heaven and earth.

Jesus came into His Kingdom the moment He ascended into Heaven and sat down next to the Father. It happened almost 2,000 years ago, in the generation in which the Disciples lived. To confirm this, read the words of Jesus in Matthew 16:28: "Truly I say to you, *there are some of those who are standing here who will not taste death until they see* the Son of Man coming in His kingdom." [Italics added]

Similarly, Mark records the words of Jesus: "There are some of those who are standing here who will not taste death until they see the kingdom of God after it has come with power." Mark 9:1

Could Jesus have said it any clearer? He declared that some of the people who were alive at that time in history would live to see Him come into His Kingdom.

Indeed, Jesus sat down on His throne 2,000 years ago. With that understanding "coming into His Kingdom," we now can look at our Lord's answer. As we look at this, do not jump to the conclusion that we reject a belief in the Second Coming. We know that Jesus will return to earth at some point in the future, and we will talk about His Second Coming later when we look at our Lord's answer to the third question. What we are saying at this point is that the Disciples' second question was not about Jesus' Second Coming, but about His coming into His Kingdom.

> Jonathan Edwards: This is evident that when Christ speaks of His coming, His being revealed, His coming in His Kingdom, or His Kingdom's coming, He has respect to His appearing in those great works of His Power, Justice and Grace, which should be in the Destruction of Jerusalem and other extraordinary Providences which should attend it. (The History of Redemption, 1199, 1776. Dec. 1, 07)

Jesus Answers The Second Question:

It is helpful to see how closely associated the destruction of Jerusalem was with the coming of Jesus into His Kingdom.

Jesus said: "But immediately after the tribulation of those days..." (Matthew 24:29) Jesus said that "immediately" after the destruction of Jerusalem, the Disciples would know that He had come into His Kingdom. He talks about that coming in the verse, which follows.

Matthew 24:30a—The Sign Of The Son Of Man

> "And then the sign of the Son of Man will appear in the sky."

Futurist teachers look at these words and envision Jesus appearing in the sky. But look carefully. Does this verse say that Jesus will appear in the sky? It says that "the sign" will appear. A sign is similar to a billboard declaring something. What is the sign? It is the sign of the Son of Man. It is not Jesus who will appear, but the sign will appear.

The King James Version of Matthew 24:30 reads like this: "And then shall appear the sign of the Son of man in heaven."

Again, careful reading leads us to see that it is not Jesus who appears, but the sign that appears. And what will that sign indicate? That the Son of Man is in Heaven. He has arrived. He has sat down on His throne. He made it!

The King James Version refers to the Son of Man in "heaven," while the New American Standard Bible (which we quoted earlier) refers to the Son of Man in the "sky." Either translation is correct because the Greek word ourano may be translated as either "heaven" or "sky." However, if we use the word "sky," the reader may envision Jesus up above in the clouds. On the other hand, if we understand that Jesus is in "Heaven," then we may envision Him with His Father sitting on His Throne.

It is this vision in Heaven that corresponds with Jesus' coming into His Kingdom. Put yourself in the shoes of the disciples 2,000 years ago sitting on the Mount of Olives.

Soon they were going to lose the One whom they had been following. He would die.

After Jesus ascended into Heaven, how were they to know that He actually had made it into Heaven?

How would they know that He had been given all authority over Heaven and earth?

That is precisely what Jesus was telling them. He was answering the question, "What will be the sign of Your coming into Your Kingdom?" And what is that sign? Jesus had just told them about all the signs that would end in the destruction of Jerusalem and the Temple.

That destruction was the sign. It was the billboard.

Once they saw the destruction of Jerusalem and the Temple, they were to know without a doubt that Jesus Christ was on His throne in Heaven.

To gain an understanding of the impact that sign had on the first-century Jewish Disciples, compare it with what happened to Japan in 1945 when two atomic bombs were dropped on Hiroshima and Nagasaki. When those bombs decimated the two cities, Japanese people watching from a distance realized that the war was over. They had lost; the United States had taken control.

Now compare that with what happened when Jerusalem was destroyed in AD 70. More people died in Jerusalem than when the two atomic bombs were dropped in Japan.

- The Jewish nation fell.
- The Temple was destroyed.
- When the Temple was destroyed, the Jewish religious system ended.
- No longer could people approach God through the Temple with animal sacrifices.
- There was a new High Priest.
- The Stone that the builders had rejected had become the Chief Cornerstone.

- There was a new Temple being built out of living stones.
- That was the sign that Jesus came into His Kingdom.
- The throne of David had been lifted to Heaven. From there Jesus Christ would rule over His Eternal Kingdom.

Matthew 24:29—The Signs Of Judgment

> "But immediately after the tribulation of those days the sun will be darkened, and the moon will not give its light, and the stars will fall from the sky, and the powers of the heavens will be shaken." NASB

To understand this passage, first notice the time frame. Jesus said that these things would happen "immediately after the tribulation of those days." Since the tribulation that Jesus described happened in AD 70, we should look for the fulfilment of this verse "immediately" after AD 70. To see this fulfilment, we need to be familiar with certain Jewish idioms. The sun, the moon, and the stars frequently were used to refer to governing authorities.

For example, Joseph had a dream in which the sun, moon, and stars all bowed down to him (Genesis 37:9); when Joseph relayed this dream to his family, they did not conclude that the sun, moon, and stars would literally bow, but that Joseph would be raised above governing authorities.

Similarly, we can read in Revelation 12:1 that a woman appears with the sun and moon under her feet and a crown of stars on her head, meaning that she had great authority.

In modern times we often use similar terminology when speaking of a movie star or a superstar. In biblical termin-ology, the fame and glory of large cities were said to shine as the sun, moon, or stars. When a certain city was destroyed, the sun, moon, or stars were said to darken. For example, in the Book of Ezekiel we can read about the judgment and coming destruction of Egypt.

> "And when I extinguish you, I will cover the heavens and darken their stars; I will cover the sun with a cloud And the moon will not give its light. 8 All the shining lights in the heavens I will

> darken over you And will set darkness on your land," Declares the Lord God. Ezekiel 32:7-8 NASB

This destruction that was prophesied by Ezekiel happened to Egypt, but there is no record of the sun, moon, and stars literally going dark. We can understand this when we realize that Prophets sometimes spoke in this apocalyptic terminology. We can compare it with modern-day idioms that people may use when tragedy strikes:

- "His life caved in around him!"
- "They pulled the rug out from under him!"
- "The sky is falling!" or "It was lights out for him when he took that punch!"

It may be difficult for modern-day Christians to think of Jesus using such terminology, but that is exactly what He did. In fact, that is the only way we find this terminology used anywhere else in the Bible (as you will see in more examples listed below). It was a Jewish idiom in reference to coming destruction and the transfer of authority. Consider how Isaiah decreed destruction upon a region south of Israel known as Edom:

> "And all the host of heaven will wear away, And the sky will be rolled up like a scroll; All their hosts will also wither away As a leaf withers from the vine, Or as one withers from the fig tree.
> 5 For My sword is satiated in heaven, Behold it shall descend for judgment upon Edom And upon the people whom I have devoted to destruction." Isaiah 34:4-5 NASB

At that time in history the sky was not literally "rolled up like a scroll." The hosts of heaven did not literally fall to the ground as leaves from a fig tree. Yet, Edom was destroyed.

Finally, consider God's declaration of judgment through Isaiah upon Babylon:

> "For the stars of heaven and their constellations Will not flash forth their light; The sun will be dark when it rises And the moon will not shed its light." Isaiah 13:10

When Babylon was judged, there was no record of stars and constellations ceasing from shining. The sun was not dark when it came up. The moon did not dim. Yet destruction came. If we are going to allow the Bible to interpret itself, we will conclude that Jesus was using apocalyptic language to declare destruction.

Just as the Prophets Isaiah and Ezekiel spoke judgments against Egypt, Edom, and Babylon, so also Jesus as a Prophet declared destruction upon Jerusalem. The Disciples of Jesus would have recognized that phraseology; they knew the Old Testament. Such terminology was part of their cultural expressions. This fits perfectly with what actually took place after Jesus died, was resurrected, and ascended into Heaven.

- Jesus sat down at the right hand of the Father.
- He was given all authority over Heaven and earth.
- The evidence on earth of Jesus ruling in Heaven was that the old Temple was destroyed.
- There was a new High Priest sitting in Heaven.
- There was a new ruler: the King of kings and the Lord of lords, who is at the right hand of God, having gone into Heaven, after angels and authorities and powers had been subjected to Him. (1 Peter 3:22)
- The heavens were shaken because Jesus Christ came into His Kingdom.

Matthew 24:30b—The Son Of Man In Glory

We have already examined the first part of Matthew 24:30; now let's consider the rest of the verse. "And then the sign of the Son of Man will appear in the sky, and then all the tribes of the earth will mourn, and they will see the Son of Man coming on the clouds of the sky with power and great glory."

What is the meaning of "then all the tribes of the earth will mourn"?

To answer this, we need to examine the Greek word ge, which has been translated in this version to "earth." When this word ge is translated in other passages of the New Testament, it is most often translated as "land." In fact, this word is often used when referring to the Promised Land of the Jews. This is what we believe is truer to the context of this Passage. Hence, we are told that all the tribes of the land shall mourn.

Who are the tribes of the land?

The land that is spoken of in this passage is the Promised Land. Therefore, all of the tribes of Israel will mourn. When news of the destruction of the Temple and the whole of Jerusalem reached the tribes of Israel, great mourning took place in their synagogues and homes.

The "sign" (the destruction of Jerusalem) caused the "tribes" (of Israel) to mourn greatly, yet they still missed the significance of the sign. It was the sign that "the Son of Man" was "in Heaven," that He had ascended to His Father.

Matthew 24:31—Angels Gathering The Elect

> "And He will send forth His angels with a great trumpet and they will gather together His elect from the four winds, from one end of the sky to the other."

To many people, this can speak only of the Second Coming of Christ at the end of history. But that is not what Jesus said it meant. Only three verses after this, He states, "this generation will not pass away until all these things take place." Jesus said that this verse was descriptive of one of the things that would happen within the span of one generation. How can we understand this?

As Jesus sat down on His throne, all authority was given to Him in Heaven and earth. Everything changed the moment Jesus came into His Kingdom. The blowing of a trumpet meant to the Jews that a royal decree was going out. And what was that decree? It was time to release the angels of God to go and gather His people from every nation. At the same time, the Disciples of Jesus were commissioned to go and preach the Gospel, making disciples of every nation. No longer was the Jewish nation the only people allowed within a covenant relationship with God. Jesus had become the Good Shepherd who was gathering His sheep from across the world.

The word "gather" is significant, for it literally means "to synagogue." Christ's messengers would be gathering people together into His new synagogue. The end of the old Temple would only help to hasten the building of the New Temple, which is the Church. It is a simple fact of history that the Church began its vigorous growth after Jerusalem fell.

Matthew 24:32-33—Know That He Is Near

> "Now learn the parable from the fig tree: when its branch has already become tender and puts forth its leaves, you know that summer is near; 33 so, you too, when you see all these things, recognize that He is near, right at the door." NASB

Jesus told the Disciples here that just as the budding of a fig tree is a sure sign that summer is near, so also these warning signs would signal the beginning of a new spiritual season—the end of the old age and the flourishing of a new one.

Our Lord's lesson of the fig tree is even more powerful if we realize that Jesus and the Disciples were sitting on the mountain, which overlooks Jerusalem and the Temple. Our Lord could have easily taken a tender branch from a nearby tree and given them the lesson to watch for the obvious signs that would indicate the destruction of Jerusalem and His coming into His Kingdom.

Some teachers of the futurist view claim that the fig tree is a symbol of Israel and that when Israel is reborn as a nation, the generation that sees it happen will also see the second coming of Christ. This is an astounding interpretation. In the Bible, Israel typically is pictured as an olive tree rather than a fig tree (e.g., Jeremiah 11:16; Romans 11:17).

Furthermore, there is no mention of a rebirth of Israel in this context. Jesus already listed all of the signs for which they were to watch, and none of them implies anything about Israel being reborn. In the context, Jesus was not talking about an event 2,000 years in the future. Jesus was answering His Disciples' questions about His coming into His Kingdom—an event that they would see in their lifetime.

We can know that the fig tree illustration was not about the future rebirth of Israel and the Second Coming of Jesus because the next verse is the Lord's declaration that all of the signs would happen in that generation (24:34). Furthermore, that would contradict what Jesus says two verses later (24:36) about there being no signs to indicate when His Second Coming would occur (a subject we will discuss shortly).

Jesus would not talk about looking at the obvious signs and then immediately say that He does not even know the day and the hour of His return.

For anyone who needs more proof, we can also know that the fig tree illustration was not about the rebirth of Israel and that generation seeing the Second Coming of Jesus, because it simply is not true!

Israel became a nation in 1948, and more than 60 years have passed without Jesus' return. The obvious, simple lesson of the fig tree was to watch for all the signs listed in Matthew 24:4-28. When those signs were fulfilled, the Disciples were to know that Jesus had come into His Kingdom.

Matthew 24:34—In This Generation

Jesus ended His answer to the Disciples' second question by saying: "Truly I say to you, this generation will not pass away until all these things take place." If we take these verses literally, then we will believe that everything Jesus prophesied in Matthew 24:5-34 was fulfilled by AD 70. Of course, futurist teachers cannot accept the words of Jesus. Sometimes they redefine the word "generation" (genesis, in Greek) to be "race," and hence, they claim that all of the events listed in Matthew 24 will happen before the race of the Jews passes away. In reality, that reinterpretation is inconsistent with the rest of the New Testament. The Greek word genesis is used 34 times in the New Testament, and never is it translated as "race" in any commonly used translation of the Bible.

If we simply accept the natural and literal meaning of Jesus' statement, we will conclude that all of the events recorded, including the coming of the Lord, happened within the lifetime of the Disciples who were listening to Jesus at that time.

> John Calvin: Christ informs them, that before a single generation shall have been completed, they will learn by experience the truth of what he has said. For within fifty years the city was destroyed and the temple was razed, the whole country was reduced to a hideous desert. (Commentary on a Harmony of the Evangelists, Matthew, Mark, and Luke, 1949, vol. 3, p. 151)

> Charles Spurgeon: The King left his followers in no doubt as to when these things should happen: "Verily I say unto you, this generation shall not pass till all these things be fulfilled." It was just about the ordinary limit of a generation when the Roman

> armies compassed Jerusalem, whose measure of iniquity was then full, and overflowed in misery, agony, distress, and bloodshed such as the world never saw before or since. Jesus was a true Prophet; everything that he foretold was literally fulfilled. (The Gospel of the Kingdom, 1974, p. 218)

Question #3: "What About The End Of The Age [World]?"

The third question the Disciples asked pertained to the end of the age (Matthew 24:3). As we mentioned earlier, the Greek word for age, aion, is translated in some Bible versions as "world," and, therefore, it may be understood that the Disciples were asking about the end of the world.

In the following discussion we will use the term "age," but the end of the age definitely will be the end of the world, as we know it.

Jesus Answers the Third Question

Jesus answered the third question of the Disciples in Matthew 24:35-25:46. Christians who have a red-letter edition of the Bible (that is an edition where all the words of Jesus are printed in red) will notice that Matthew 24:35-25:46 are all the words of Jesus. It is one long discourse in which Jesus answers the question about the end of the age.

We will go through these verses passage by passage, but first it is important to identify how we know that Matthew 24:35 is where Jesus begins answering the third question. We did not arbitrarily choose this as the verse in which He began, but a quick examination of the Scriptures reveals that this is, indeed, where Jesus started talking about the end of the age. Allow us to explain.

We already studied Matthew 24:34, where Jesus said that everything preceding that verse would happen in that generation. He was giving a notable break and a reasonable place for us to see how the events after Matthew 24:34 could happen at a later date, in a later generation. Further, we can note the next verse, where Jesus begins answering the third question: "Heaven and earth will pass away, but My words will not pass away." (Matthew 24:35)

Jesus is emphasizing how His words certainly will come true, but He is also making a statement about the end of things—heaven and earth passing away. That is what the Disciples asked in their third question: "What about the end of the age (world)?"

Finally, we can know that this is where Jesus began answering the third question because He starts talking about the "day and hour": "But of that day and hour no one knows, not even the angels of heaven, nor the Son, but the Father alone." (Matthew 24:36)

When the Bible uses the terminology "the day and hour," or "the Great Day," or "the last day," or in some contexts "the day," it refers to judgment day, and not just any judgment day, but the final great judgment day when God will call all people to account at the end of the world (e.g., Matthew 7:22; Luke 10:12; John 6:39; 12:48; Romans 2:16; 1 Corinthians 1:8; 3:13; 5:5; Philippians 1:6; 1:10; 2 Thessalonians 1:10; 2 Timothy 1:18; 4:8; Hebrews 10:25; 2 Peter 3:10, 12; Jude 1:6).

That final great judgment day is the topic of the rest of Matthew 24 and all of Matthew 25. Jesus compares the great judgment day with the judgment of Noah's flood (Matthew 24:37-39)

- Two men in a field (24:40-41),
- A thief coming in the night (24:42-44),
- A master returning to demand that his servants give an accounting (24:45-51),
- A groom returning for his bride (25:1-13),
- And a master returning to see how his servants have used their talents (25:14-30).

Jesus ends this great teaching by talking about the Son of Man coming in glory with all of the angels, and then the nations being gathered before Him (Matthew 25:31-46).

We briefly will examine each of these passages, but notice that each talks about the coming judgment and the returning Judge. Hence, we understand that Jesus is answering the third question concerning the end of the age (or world).

> Charles Spurgeon: There is a manifest change in our Lord's words here, which clearly indicate that they refer to His last great coming to judgment. (The Gospel of the Kingdom, 1974, p. 218)

Matthew 24:36—No One Knows When

> "But of that day and hour no one knows, not even the angels of heaven, nor the Son, but the Father alone."

The key point of this passage is that the Day of the Lord will be a surprise. Jesus does not know when it will come.

The angels do not know. Only the Father knows. Jesus went on to explain that it will come with no warning.

Notice how different our Lord's answer is to this question than to the other two questions. Concerning the destruction of Jerusalem, Jesus said that there would be time to preach the Gospel, and then armies would surround Jerusalem.

Concerning our Lord's coming into His Kingdom, Jesus said that the primary visible sign would be the destruction of Jerusalem and the Temple. However, concerning the end of the age, Jesus said, "no one knows, not even the angels of Heaven, nor the Son." This surprise element of the end of the age is a fundamental theme of each of the parables that Jesus gave in the rest of Matthew Chapter 24 and all of Matthew Chapter 25.

Matthew 24:37-39—As The Days Of Noah

> "For the coming of the Son of Man will be just like the days of Noah. 38 For as in those days before the flood they were eating and drinking, marrying and giving in marriage, until the day that Noah entered the ark, 39 and they did not understand until the flood came and took them all away; so will the coming of the Son of Man be."

Jesus wanted to impress upon the Disciples' minds (and our minds) that the final Day of Judgment would come as a surprise. Just as in Noah's day, people will be eating and drinking, marrying and giving in marriage; then suddenly Jesus will appear, and judgment day will have arrived.

Matthew 24:40-42: As Two Men In A Field

> "Then there will be two men in the field; one will be taken and one will be left. Two women will be grinding at the mill; one will be taken and one will be left. Therefore be on the alert, for you do not know which day your Lord is coming."

The primary point of this Passage is that the great judgment day will come suddenly, and therefore, people should always be alert.

Matthew 24:43-44—As A Thief In The Night

Next, Jesus taught the surprise element with a parable of a thief coming in the night.

> "But be sure of this, that if the head of the house had known at what time of the night the thief was coming, he would have been on the alert and would not have allowed his house to be broken into. 44 For this reason you also must be ready; for the Son of Man is coming at an hour when you do not think He will."

Not only will the great judgment day arrive without warning, but it will also come when we do not expect it. Therefore, be ready at all times.

Matthew 24:45-51—As A Master Returning

> "Who then is the faithful and sensible slave whom his master put in charge of his household to give them their food at the proper time? 46 Blessed is that slave whom his master finds so doing when he comes. 47 Truly I say to you that he will put him in charge of all his possessions. 48 But if that evil slave says in his heart, 'My master is not coming for a long time,' 49 and begins to beat his fellow slaves and eat and drink with drunkards; 50 the master of that slave will come on a day when he does not expect him and at an hour which he does not know, 51 and will cut him in pieces and assign him a place with the hypocrites; in that place there will be weeping and gnashing of teeth."

There are many lessons that can be taken from this Passage, but the most fundamental truth is that judgment day will arrive as a surprise with no warning, and therefore, the listener is exhorted to continue being diligent in service and living righteously.

Matthew 25:1-13—As Ten Virgins Waiting

In the next Passage, Jesus told a parable of 10 virgins who were waiting for their groom to come and take them. Five of the virgins were foolish, not ready for the return of the groom, while the other five were wise, staying prepared for the groom. The most obvious lesson, again, is that God's people must be ready because Jesus could return at any time without warning.

Matthew 25:14-30—As Servants With Talents

Jesus then offered a parable about a man entrusting his possessions to three servants. To one he gave five talents! To another two! And to the last servant one talent! When the master returned, he demanded that each servant give an account of how he had used the talents. Then he rewarded them each accordingly.

The primary lesson of coming judgment is so obvious that we do not need to comment. A secondary lesson is that there would be a great delay before the return of Christ. We see that delay in verse 19, which says: "Now after *a long time* the master of those slaves came." This delay is unlike the judgment upon Jerusalem, which was to happen in that generation.

Matthew 25:31-46—The Great Day of Judgment

In the final passage of Matthew Chapter 25, Jesus gave a description and summary of the coming great day of judgment.

> "But when the Son of Man comes in His glory, and all the angels with Him, then He will sit on His glorious throne. 32 All the nations will be gathered before Him; and He will separate them from one another, as the shepherd separates the sheep from the goats; 33 and He will put the sheep on His right, and the goats on the left. 34 Then the King will say to those on His right, 'Come, you who are blessed of My Father, inherit the kingdom…' 41 Then

He will also say to those on His left, 'Depart from Me, accursed ones, into the eternal fire...' 46 These will go away into eternal punishment, but the righteous into eternal life."

Again, The Lesson Is Clear: Jesus Will Return To Judge The Righteous And The Unrighteous.

The third question that the Disciples asked—"What about the end of the age?"—Jesus clearly answered.

[17]Summary

A significant portion of the Body of Christ around the world holds the understanding of Matthew 24, which I have just presented to you.

The reason I mention this is to make it clear that we have not presented some bizarre doctrine that no one else believes. Thousands of Bible teachers would explain Matthew Chapter 24 similarly to the way I have just explained it.

If you really understand Matthew Chapter 24, then you will embrace many ideas that may be new to you, the most important point being that there will be no signs preceding the Second Coming of Jesus or the end of the world. Jesus did not know of any signs, and no one else will be able to figure it out either.

Jesus was emphatic about this point, giving no less than six different parables to make sure His followers would understand that it will be a total surprise to everyone except the Father.

This is contradictory to what is spoken of by futurist teachers, who love to create in their listeners, anticipation of the Second Coming by talking about:

- Increasing wars,
- Famines,
- Earthquakes,
- False religious leaders,
- And people falling away from the faith.

17 For more on this important subject, I would like to recommend the book "Victorious Eschatology", which can be purchased at: worldcastministries.com/books/victorious-eschatology-second-edition/

In reality, all of those signs preceded the destruction of Jerusalem in AD 70. When Jesus returns at some point in the future, you will be eating and drinking, driving your car, sleeping in bed, or working at your job. Then suddenly Jesus Christ will appear in the sky. No warning, no signs.

It is very evident and clear that what many have accepted as truth for so long concerning what the Scriptures say regarding Jesus and the end-time has been inaccurate and false. We must let the Scriptures interpret Scriptures otherwise we would continue to witness more false prophecies concerning the end of the world and the return of Jesus. We have to be like the Bereans in Apostle Paul's day and search the Scriptures carefully and thoroughly for truth—present truth!

> "Now the Berean Jews were of more noble character than those in Thessalonica, for they received the message with great eagerness and examined the Scriptures every day to see if what Paul said was true." Acts 17:11 NIV

In the next chapter we would be carefully examining what the Scriptures really say about the two sons that Abraham had and how they impact the Church—the Body of Believers in Jesus Christ today. Once again, please let us be like the Bereans and have your Bible and let us take this journey together.

CHAPTER SEVEN

UNDERSTANDING GALATIANS CHAPTER 4

Galatians Chapter 4 presents one of the clearest writings and teachings concerning the Old and New Covenants and the reasons as to why we need to fully understand the differences. Chapter 4 continues from 3:26-29 with a very important opening few verses that highlights a very important issue, which we must first clarify and understand before we go forward. Here is what Apostle Paul says:

> "For you are all sons of God through faith in Christ Jesus.
> 27 For as many of you as were baptized into Christ have put
> on Christ. 28 There is neither Jew nor Greek, there is neither
> slave nor free, there is neither male nor female; for you are all
> one in Christ Jesus. 29 *And if you are Christ's, then you are*
> *Abraham's seed, and heirs according to the promise*." [Italics
> added] Galatians 3:26-29

> "Now I say that *the heir, as long as he is a child, does not differ*
> *at all from a slave*, though he is master of all, 2 but is under
> guardians and stewards until the time appointed by the father.

> 3 Even so we, when we were children, were in bondage under the elements of the world. 4 But when the fullness of the time had come, God sent forth His Son, born of a woman, born under the law, 5 to redeem those who were under the law, that we might receive the adoption as sons. 6 And because you are sons, God has sent forth the Spirit of His Son into your hearts, crying out, "Abba, Father!" 7 Therefore you are no longer a slave but a son, and if a son, then an heir of God through Christ." [Italics added] Galatians 4:1-7

In this passage of Scripture there are two words for the English word "son", which are:

- Teknon, which is used to describe an offspring who does not posses or exhibit the qualities of his father; he is referred to as a child, and as such is no different than a slave.
- Huios, which is used to describe one who has and exhibits all the nature and qualities of his Father.

For example when we read in Matthew 5:9, 44-45 it is very important to understand that huios is used for sons and not teknon!

> "Blessed *are* the peacemakers, For they shall be called sons [huios] of God... 44 But I say to you, love your enemies, bless those who curse you, do good to those who hate you, and pray for those who spitefully use you and persecute you, 45 that you may be sons [huios] of your Father in heaven; for He makes His sun rise on the evil and on the good, and sends rain on the just and on the unjust." [Parenthesis added]

In 1 Corinthians 13:11 we see these two dimensions (of teknon and huios) being clearly depicted:

> "When I was a child [huios], I spoke as a child [huios], I understood as a child [huios], I thought as a child [huios]; but when I became a man [mature son—teknon], I put away childish things." [Parenthesis added]

In chapter one of this book we briefly mentioned the difference between Vashti [Old Order System—Israel] and Esther (New Order System—Church). In this chapter I would like for us to go a bit deeper in our understanding of these two women/systems and draw out some much needed truth.

OLD ORDER—LAW	NEW ORDER—GRACE
Bondwoman of Galatians 4	Freewoman of Galatians 4
Cain	Abel
Hagar	Sarah
Leah	Rachel
Peninnah	Hannah
Naomi	Ruth
Vashti (Israel)	Esther (Church)
Earthly Jerusalem	Heavenly Jerusalem
Old Covenant	New Covenant
Bondage	Freedom/Liberty
Law of sin and death	Law of the Spirit of Life
Harlot of Revelation 17-18	Bride of Revelation 19

Once we have accepted Jesus Christ as our Saviour and Lord and we have entered into His Life we now have a new identity. Please understand this very important fact, if you have no identity, or do not know your identity you cannot enter fully into your priesthood as a Believer!

Let me briefly share with you a couple areas of identity that I believe are critical for every Believer to accept, understand and walk in.

1. We are Priests and Kings:
We are ruling priests and kings, according to Revelation 1:5-6, 5:8-10.

"Grace to you and peace from Him who is and who was and who is to come, and from the seven Spirits who are before His throne, 5 and from Jesus Christ, the faithful witness, the firstborn from the dead, and the ruler over the kings of the earth. To Him who loved us and washed us from our sins in His

> own blood, 6 *and has made us kings and priests* to His God and Father, to Him be glory and dominion forever and ever. Amen." [Italics added]

> "Now when He had taken the scroll, the four living creatures and the twenty-four elders fell down before the Lamb, each having a harp, and golden bowls full of incense, which are the prayers of the saints. 9 And they sang a new song, saying: "You are worthy to take the scroll, And to open its seals; For You were slain, And have redeemed us to God by Your blood Out of every tribe and tongue and people and nation, 10 *And have made us kings and priests to our God*; And we shall reign on the earth." [Italics added]

2. We are Sons of God:

As revealed to us in Romans Chapter 8—the whole of Chapter 8 deals with the authority, the right and the privilege of being a Son of God. Being a Son of God is a new class in Christ and it is *not gender specific*. Your status as a Son of God is not eroded or defined by whether or not you are educated, rich or poor, on the mountain top or not. You are a Son of God because this is who Christ has called us to be!

I would like to spend some time in the next few pages of this book making an attempt to bring some light or understanding to the different dimensions of Sonship in God!

Galatians 3:26-28 makes a very poignant point in declaring that we are all Sons of God once we are Born-Again. We do not have to do anything except get saved and when that occurs we are known as Sons of God.

> "For you are all sons of God through faith in Christ Jesus. 27 For as many of you as were baptized into Christ have put on Christ. 28 There is neither Jew nor Greek, there is neither slave nor free, there is neither male nor female; for you are all one in Christ Jesus."

When we submit ourselves to the Spirit of the Lord, as His Sons, we are changed in person; we are now conformed to the image and likeness of Jesus Christ. The Book of Romans Chapter 8 gives us some vital and valid information concerning how this is accomplished and as such I would like for us to take a journey through its verses.

We will begin in Romans 8:1 "There is therefore now *no condemnation* to those who are in Christ Jesus, who do not walk according to the flesh, but according to the Spirit." [Italics added]

No Condemnation

The English word condemnation is derived from a Greek word "katakrima," that means: a judgement that is spoken against you after careful examination of your circumstances. Many Believers today walk around with the sentence of condemnation as the enemy has made a careful examination of their situation and is seeking to bring a sentence or judgement against them. However, the Word of God is specific in classifying those who experience *no condemnation*; and they are those:

- Who are *in* Christ
- Who do not walk according to the flesh
- Who walk according to the Spirit

Walk

The word walk is translated from a Greek word peripateo, which means to conduct yourself in life or to set a course for your life's progress. It does not mean that you have to become spooky or to experience a continual anointing that gives you *Goosebumps*. It refers to a normal, healthy, Biblical lifestyle.

Romans 8:5 gives a valuable key about walking in the Spirit. It encourages us to set our mind to behave in a certain way for successful living. In essence if you set your mind on the things of the flesh then you will walk in the flesh, but if you set your mind on the things of the Spirit then you will walk in the Spirit. However, if you walk in the flesh there is condemnation and if you walk in the Spirit there is *no condemnation*!

> "For those who live according to the flesh *set their minds* on the things of the flesh, but those who live according to the Spirit, the things of the Spirit." [Italics added]

Set Your Mind

In the Greek this word "phroneó" means—to strive, to be in phase with; and actually carries two meanings, which are:

- To be in harmony with, to be on the same musical sound or to be on the same wavelength or frequency! In essence both the fleshly realm and the Spirit realm have frequencies, right here and now.
- To strive for or to seek strongly.

One has to strive to be in synch with the Spirit as it does not come naturally. There is a *walking in the Spirit* that we must do if we are to master and conquer this life. So let us read Romans 8:5 again for emphasis—"They who are constantly striving to be in phase with the flesh will walk according to the flesh; but they who strive to be in phase or harmony with the Spirit will walk in the Spirit."

The next powerful thing that we see is in Romans 8:2-4. Here we read and understand that Jesus came in the likeness of sinful flesh.

> "For the law of the Spirit of life in Christ Jesus has made me free from the law of sin and death. 3 For what the law could not do in that it was weak through the flesh, *God did by sending His own Son in the likeness of sinful flesh*, on account of sin: He condemned sin in the flesh, 4 *that the righteous requirement of the law might be fulfilled in us* who do not walk according to the flesh but according to the Spirit." [Italics added]

What exactly does it mean 'in the likeness of sinful flesh'? Jesus, Himself was not sinful flesh but He came as close to sinful flesh as He could without actually sinning so that He could present the best model for man to see and live by. Now the question is why did He do that? I believe the answer is, that the righteousness of the Law might be fulfilled in us; who walk according to the Spirit and not according to the flesh. The Law was righteous but its requirement condemned all under sin, and only Jesus completely fulfilled all its requirements; so through Him we have fulfilled all the requirements of the Law! We do not have to become "a spirit" for that to happen, no, we could walk and operate in the Spirit, while still in our fleshly bodies! *Hallelujah*!

Another interesting word that is found in the aforementioned text is the word *fulfilled*; which carries the following meaning from the Greek word "pleroo," which means, "to fill up completely to overflowing." There was a righteous requirement of the Law that could not be fulfilled without Christ and a conscious walking in the Spirit.

What was the righteous requirement of the Law? The Law demanded perfection and righteousness, but could not provide for it. This was so because no matter what they did ceremonially, the High Priest had to go back into the Holy of Holies every year; to atone for the people, unlike the Blood of Jesus that was shed once to atone for the sins of the entire world. This is very powerful; Jesus' Blood that was shed over Two Thousand years ago was shed for everyone living at the time and also everyone else that has been born since and that will ever be born until His return! This is simply—*Awesome*! We have now fulfilled the righteous requirement of the Law because of the finished work of Jesus Christ and our walk in His Spirit! You and I are Sons of God and we have fulfilled the Law! Isn't that good news? *Yes it is good news*!

In Romans 8:14 the Holy Spirit brings to light a very important and powerful fact. It says: "For *as many as are led by the Spirit of God, these are sons of God*." [Italics added]

If we were to follow the original construct of this verse, this is how it should read: "As many as are led by the Spirit they are the (*operational*) sons of God." So this identifies two things:

- Once you are Born Again you are *potentially* a Son of God; because the verse implies that one could be Born Again and not allow oneself to be *led* by the Holy Spirit.
- You can function as an *operational* son if you submit yourself to be *led* by the Holy Spirit!

Led implies that choices have to be made. So then, as a result, when we use the term *operational son* what we are speaking about is making accurate choices in life—"as many as are *led* by the Spirit they are the (*operational*) sons of God!"

Here are a few examples of what I would call operational sons in both the Old and New Testaments. In the Old Testament we read of a man named Enoch. [18]Enoch, was translated into God's presence

18 Hebrews 11:5

without experiencing death because it was recorded that he pleased God; in essence he was a Son of God. He was one who made correct choices every day of his life. I like how the writer of Genesis talks about Enoch in Genesis 5:24 "And Enoch walked with God; and he was not, for God took him."

Again in the Old Testament we read of [19]Moses, who made a choice to suffer affliction with his people rather than continue to live as Pharaoh's son. What an incredible decision. This man was a son of Pharaoh with all the trimmings and trappings of that lifestyle, and when the time came for him to choose, [20]he made the accurate choice and as such became a Son of God.

What can be said about Abraham in the Old Testament who left all his wealthy, affluent lifestyle to go on a journey to find the City of God? His incredible choice led him to being known as the father of faith and he was also known as a friend of God—(James 2:23).

So in essence we are seeking to understand how we need to operate as sons in the midst of the challenges of life, without compromising our Christ-like identity! And one of the ways that we can accomplish this and to stand strong and steadfast is to be truly *led* by the Holy Spirit!

To be led means to point and accompany one towards a specific destination. The word led also means to direct and to guide; to move one forward by applying an influence to the mind! To be led by the Spirit is to allow the Holy Spirit to influence your mind so that He will cause you to arrive at the pre-determined destination. For example here are some very elementary situations that can be applied to the word "led," so that we get a clearer understanding. Sometimes we can become so deep and spiritually focused that we forget that the Holy Spirit is intimately involved in our "everyday lives" or should I say the "everydayness of our lives". And yes, He is interested in what we may consider to be the simple, little, insignificant things about our lives; such as:

- Going to the bank to deal with an unpaid loan…
- Getting upset with an unscrupulous boss…
- Dealing with a rebellious teenager…
- Working through a broken relationship…
- Knowing whether to buy or sell property at any given time…

---

19 Exodus 2:10
20 Hebrews 11:24

And being led of the Spirit can also range to the more complex issue of life such as knowing the accurate timings in God when certain moves that can have significant and eternal consequences need to be made. Here is a fitting example in the life of Jesus that I find to be rather intriguing and also at the same time very encouraging.

Jesus' entry into Jerusalem is one of those situations that I find rather intriguing and also at the same time very encouraging and I refer to it often. As their custom was, every year Jesus had to make the journey up to Jerusalem. On one such occasion we read about Jesus as a twelve year old boy who became separated from his parents on the journey but was found in the Temple where He confounded the doctors and lawyers that were present at the time—Luke 2:41-45.

Now in the Gospel according to John Chapter 7 we read that the Feast of Tabernacles was at hand and Jesus made a decision not to go to the Feast of Tabernacles because as He put it in John 7:6-8; "His time had not yet come." However, when His time had come and Jesus knew it by the Spirit; as such He was able to reveal it to His Disciples and therefore made the journey, which resulted in His death. The point here is this, had He not chosen to be led by the Spirit and chose the accurate time to go to Jerusalem our salvation would have been in jeopardy; as it depended on Jesus becoming the Perfect Sacrifice at the perfect time.

In situations of such a complex nature and sometimes because of all the uncertainty connected to these scenarios, dialogue is so important! As a leader I cannot be impulsive; I must think things through and not always jump on the spur of the moment! Being *led* of the Spirit is *long term* and very rarely it is the spur of the moment or short-term decisions and directions. That's why there is no room for discouragement because your present state is not your destination!—Therefore, *be led by the Spirit*!

Romans 8:14-15 continues by declaring to us that we have been adopted. This idea of adoption literally identifies someone shifting from one place to another, and not merely some concept. If we have been adopted, we have been literally shifted from one place to another. Because of this adoption we can cry Abba Father!

This word Abba in Scripture is not what most people declared it to be for so long, saying that it means a friendly or familiar Name for Father God. This word was literally used as a sacred Name for God. When the Jews prayed they used this word, and it was not to be used by servants or slaves. However, this word was used so very often that in Christian circles they developed it to mean a familiar term for God (like daddy). The word used for Father in this context is the word pater, which is rendered "a father operating on an earthly sphere".

In light of this, what the Apostle Paul was saying is that we as Born-again, Spirit-filled Believers have been given the Spirit of adoption as sons which means we can now enter into the sacred realm of the Heavens and touch God. Because we can cry Abba, (the sacred and most holy and revered Name for God) and we can also cry Father, causing us to also function on the earth with Him as pater—father. Both the sacred and earthly dimensions are given to us!

God is both Sacred and Eternal and a living Father in your everyday circumstances upon the earth. You can bridge the gap between Heaven and earth. *This is what it means to be a son.* We can touch the sacredness of God without fear and still function on the earth and not become weird or downright spooky!

Again, Apostle Paul in writing to the Galatians brings to light a very important distinction when explaining our adoption as sons. Beginning in Galatians 4:1, he identifies three levels for the Believer: child, slave and heir or son. As long as the son is a child he is no different than a slave.

The devil has tried for a long time to convince the Believer to see him or herself as a child/slave, regardless of the fact that we are an heir and joint heirs with Christ. If we buy into that child/slave mentality and never grow up into Sonship, Believers will deal with the things of Father as slaves. Do we need to cultivate and function in the mentality of a Son? Absolutely! The reason being that in Galatians 4:3 there is a very important or key principle, which states: "As children you were in bondage under the *elements of this world*." [Italics added]

Elements Of This World

That word "element" is derived from the Greek word "stoichos," which means: a row, rank, series or a staircase. In order for a staircase to work you must have the first "stair tread" or step otherwise it will not function the way it was intended to. This word "stoichos" also means the first principles of life, or basic foundation. It also means something that takes its elevation from the principle before it. So in essence the world system is built from an ascending order of principles; everything is linked up to something else to get you more tied up. Jesus was sent to break us free from these elements of the world that we walked in as children so that we would enter fully into our position as sons where we can cry Abba Father and break from the slave mentality.

Remember that there are three types of persons that have been identified in Galatians Chapter 4: the child, the slave and the heir or son. The child is identified as one who is still under [21]bondage to the elements of this world or the world's system of operation. The slave is identified as one who is in servitude and has no ranking. The slave has no one to command and is the lowest in the chain of command. In this context you are a son but you have a child's mentality and cannot and will not enter into your true privileges. You are like a member of the *royal family* and instead of dining with the royal family at dinner and using the expensive chinaware at your disposal, you keep dining with the servants and possibly using disposable serving trays. You cannot exercise any authority with a childish or slavish mentality. The heir or son is identified as one who has the authority and knows who he is as the possessor of all things. He knows his identity! Galatians 4:6 identifies something very powerful: "And because you are sons, God has sent forth the Spirit of His Son into your hearts, crying out, "Abba, Father!" Awesome! Because you are a son, you can use the Sacred Name of Abba. You should no longer think like a slave who is not allowed to use the Name "Abba!"

Our Sonship in Christ is not a new concept or something that was born in the New Testament; no, this is what the Lord God always intended. Let's journey a bit further into Galatians 4 to focus on a few vital things.

In this Chapter the Apostle Paul was presenting irrefutable evidence to the fact that God always intended to have a people for Himself and that we the *Born-Again Believers* are that people. Hear me this was always His intention! Everything that occurred before Jesus Christ came died, and rose again from the dead (which resulted in our

21 Ephesians 2:1-2 vs. Hebrews 5:12, 6:1 Principles of Christ

Salvation through Him) were all types and shadows leading up to that point. The Apostle Paul makes this comprehensively clear in Galatians 4:9-21, and then he further drives the point home in Galatians 4:22-31.

> "For it is written that Abraham had two sons: the one by a bondwoman, the other by a freewoman. 23 But he who was of the bondwoman was born according to the flesh, and he of the freewoman through promise, 24 *which things are symbolic*. For *these are the two covenants*: the one from Mount Sinai which gives birth to bondage, which is Hagar-- 25 for this Hagar is Mount Sinai in Arabia, and corresponds to Jerusalem which now is, and is in bondage with her children-- 26 but the Jerusalem above is free, which is the mother of us all. 27 For it is written: "Rejoice, O barren, You who do not bear! Break forth and shout, You who are not in labour! For the desolate has many more children Than she who has a husband." 28 *Now we, brethren, as Isaac was, are children of promise*. 29 But, as he who was born according to the flesh then persecuted him who was born according to the Spirit, even so it is now. 30 Nevertheless what does the Scripture say? "Cast out the bondwoman and her son, for the son of the bondwoman shall not be heir with the son of the freewoman." 31 *So then, brethren, we are not children of the bondwoman but of the free*." [Italics added] Galatians 4:22-31

Verse 28 declares: "Now we, brethren, as Isaac was, are children of promise..." There are a few things I want to share concerning this:

- Abraham had two sons: one by the slave or bondwoman who bore Ishmael, and one by the free woman who bore Isaac.
- Ishmael represents religious bondage and Isaac represents the true sons of God.
- Remember, that Ishmael and the other children that Abraham had with his concubines all got "gifts" but the Covenant made with him by God was established with Isaac, he got everything his father Abraham owned—Genesis 17:18-22; Genesis 25:5-6.

As was shown in the chart between the Old Covenant and the New Covenant at the beginning of this chapter, there have always been two dimensions if you will—the flesh and the spirit—the earthly and the heavenly. And as we shall see, the earthly/fleshly always seeks to persecute the heavenly/spiritual.

The Two Jerusalems

The Bible clearly speaks about the existence of [22]two Jerusalems (two cities), as well as two temples. Our understanding of which one of them is being referred to in any passage of Scripture will give us a much better understanding of what the Lord is saying. The first Jerusalem is earthly and physical, while the second is heavenly and spiritual. And both temples go by the term "Temple." It is for us to know which one is being discussed in any portion of Scripture.

Not only did the glory depart from the temple, but He also forsook Jerusalem itself. Why, then, does Scripture prophesy also of the restoration of Jerusalem? Jerusalem in Scripture is always written in the plural. It is "*Ieru shalayim*," "Jerusalems." While the ancient rabbis discussed this fact, they never understood that there were two Jerusalems. There was the old city of Jerusalem, and there was the New Jerusalem, revealed in the New Testament by men who understood the difference.

Apostle Paul spoke of this in Galatians 4:24-31, telling us that the earthly Jerusalem was "Hagar" and incapable of bringing forth the promises of God. The Jerusalem that is from above, however, is Sarah, and is "our mother," the mother of Believers in Christ.

The earthly city known as Jerusalem could no more bring forth the promised seed (Isaac is known as a type of Jesus Christ) than could Hagar. Earthly Jerusalem only brought bondage, not liberty in Christ. The end of earthly Jerusalem is found in Galatians 4:30.

> "But what does the Scripture say? "Cast out the bondwoman and her son, for the son of the bondwoman shall NOT be an heir with the son of the free woman." NASB

The clear message of the entire Book of Galatians is the fact that the Old city of Jerusalem can never bring forth the promise of God. Hagar can never bring forth Isaac. Hagar is only the mother of Ishmael,

---

22 Taken from a chapter in Daniel's Seventy Weeks By Dr. Stephen E. Jones

who never was intended to inherit the promises even though he is the son of Abram, whose name was later changed to Abraham the man who brought forth the promised seed in Isaac. Throughout the Old Testament we find countless prophecies about "Jerusalem," or "*Yerushalayim*". Sometimes they are positive, and other times negative. For a negative example, we read in Jeremiah 19:1-2.

> "Thus says the Lord, Go and buy a potter's earthenware jar, and take some of the elders of the people and some of the senior priests. 2 Then go out to the valley of Ben-hinnom [e.i., *gehenna*] and proclaim there the words that I shall tell you." [Parenthesis added] NASB

The Prophet was then told to pronounce judgment upon the city and its inhabitants—Jeremiah 19:10-12.

> "Then you are to break the jar in the sight of the men who accompany you 11 and say to them, Thus says the Lord of hosts, Just so shall I break this people and this city, even as one breaks a potter's vessel, which cannot again be repaired; and they will bury them in Topheth ["burning"] because there is no other place for burial. 12 This is how I shall treat this place [Jerusalem] and its inhabitants, declares the Lord, so as to make this city like Topheth." [Parenthesis added] NASB

When we compare this prophecy of Jerusalem to the earlier prophecy given to the House of Israel in Jeremiah 18:1-10, the comparison is even more startling. The northern House of Israel had already been carried captive into Assyria a century earlier, and yet Jeremiah prophesies that they would be like a jar of wet clay, which would be remade into another vessel.

> "The word which came to Jeremiah from the Lord saying, 2 "Arise and go down to the potter's house, and there I will announce My words to you." 3 Then I went down to the potter's house, and there he was, making something on the wheel. 4 But the vessel that he was making of clay was spoiled

> in the hand of the potter; so he remade it into another vessel, as it pleased the potter to make. 5 Then the word of the Lord came to me saying, 6 "Can I not, O house of Israel, deal with you as this potter does?" declares the Lord. "Behold, like the clay in the potter's hand, so are you in My hand, O house of Israel. 7 At one moment I might speak concerning a nation or concerning a kingdom to uproot, to pull down, or to destroy it; 8 if that nation against which I have spoken turns from its evil, I will relent concerning the calamity I planned to bring on it. 9 Or at another moment I might speak concerning a nation or concerning a kingdom to build up or to plant it; 10 if it does evil in My sight by not obeying My voice, then I will think better of the good with which I had promised to bless it." NASB

But Jerusalem was like a jar that had already been hardened. Once it was broken, it could not be repaired and could only be thrown into the city dump, referred to as the valley of the son of Hinnom. In the Greek the city dump/the valley of the son of Hinnom is called *gehenna*, (hell), which is also mentioned in the New Testament.

[23]Gehenna

In the synoptic Gospels Jesus uses the word *Gehenna* eleven times to describe the opposite to life in the Kingdom (Mark 9:43-48). It is a place where both soul and body could be destroyed (Matthew 10:28) in "unquenchable fire" (Mark 9:43). Gehenna is also mentioned in the Epistle of James 3:6, where it is said to set the tongue on fire, and the tongue in turn sets on fire the entire "course" or "wheel" of life. The complete list of references is as follows:

- Matthew 5:22: "...whoever shall say, "You fool," shall be guilty enough to go into the, 'Gehenna.'"
- Matthew 5:29: "...it is better for you that one of the parts of your body perish, than for your whole body to be thrown into, 'Gehenna.'"
- Matthew 5:30: "...better for you that one of the parts of your body perish, than for your whole body to go into, 'Gehenna.'"

23 Referenced from http://en.wikipedia.org/wiki/Gehenna

- Matthew 10:28: "...rather fear Him who is able to destroy both soul and body in, 'Gehenna.'"
- Matthew 18:9: "It is better for you to enter life with one eye, than with two eyes to be thrown into the, 'Gehenna.'"
- Matthew 23:15: "Woe to you, scribes and Pharisees, hypocrites, because you... make one proselyte... twice as much a child of 'Gehenna' as yourselves."
- Matthew 23:33, to the Pharisees: "You serpents, you brood of vipers, how shall you to escape the sentence of, 'Gehenna'?"
- Mark 9:43: "It is better for you to enter life crippled, than having your two hands, to go into, 'Gehenna,' into the unquenchable fire."
- Mark 9:45: "It is better for you to enter life lame, than having your two feet, to be cast into, 'Gehenna.'"
- Mark 9:47: "It is better for you to enter the Kingdom of God with one eye, than having two eyes, to be cast into, 'Gehenna.'"
- Luke 12:5: "...fear the One who, after He has killed has authority to cast into, 'Gehenna;' yes, I tell you, fear Him."
- James 3:6: "And the tongue is a fire... and sets on fire the course of our life, and is set on fire by, 'Gehenna.'"

The point of the contrast is to show that while Israel was given good promises of restoration, even after its long history of idolatry, Judah was not given a similar promise. In fact, there is not one word of hope given to Judah and Jerusalem in the entire passage of Jeremiah 18-19.

Jerusalem, of course, was destroyed by Nebuchadnezzar in the days of Jeremiah's prophecy. However, it was later rebuilt by Nehemiah. It was destroyed again in AD 70 by the Romans, but it was later rebuilt. It was destroyed during the Middle Ages during the Crusades, but it was always rebuilt. The city thus stands today as a city rebuilt many times over the centuries.

Jeremiah, however, prophesies of a destruction of the physical city of Jerusalem in which it can never again be repaired or rebuilt—Jeremiah 19:10-11 "Then you shall break the flask in the sight of the men who go with you, 11 and say to them, 'Thus says the LORD of hosts: "Even so I will break this people and this city, as *one* breaks a potter's vessel, which cannot be made whole again; and they shall bury *them* in Tophet till *there is* no place to bury." That prophecy has yet to be fulfilled, and so it can only happen in the future (as of this writing). But this speaks only of the old physical city. It does not speak of the New Jerusalem of Revelation 21:2, or the "Heavenly Jerusalem" of Hebrews 12:22.

Isaiah 62 also speaks of "Jerusalem" in glowing terms that appear to contradict the prophecies of Jeremiah.

> "For Zion's sake I will not keep silent, and for Jerusalem's sake I will not keep quiet, until her righteousness goes forth like brightness, and her salvation like a torch that is burning, 2 And the nations will see your righteousness, and all kings your glory; and you will be called by a new name, which the mouth of the Lord will designate." NASB

Isaiah goes on to describe this "Jerusalem" in heavenly terms. John interprets this for us in the Book of Revelation, showing that Isaiah was speaking of the New Jerusalem. Isaiah 62:5 calls the city a "bride," and John does the same in Revelation 21:2. Isaiah 60:18 says that the "walls" of Jerusalem are *salvation*, and its "gates" are *praise*. These terms describe the New Jerusalem, not the old.

Isaiah 50:19-20 says that "Jerusalem" will have no need for the sun or moon to give it light, because God Himself will be its light. John says the same of the New Jerusalem in Revelation 21:23.

> "The city has no need of the sun or the moon to shine upon it, for the glory of God has illumined it, and its lamp is the Lamb." NASB

Likewise, Isaiah speaks of the inhabitants of Jerusalem as being entirely righteous, in contrast to Jeremiah's prophecy.

We read in Isaiah 62:21 "Then all your people will be righteous." NASB. And later, John says in Revelation 21:27

> "And nothing unclean and no one who practices abomination and lying shall ever come into it, but only those whose names are written in the Lamb's book of life." NASB

A simple comparison of Isaiah and Revelation makes it clear that neither Prophet was talking about the old Jerusalem, but about the New One. Of course, Judaism rejects the New Testament and because of this, they do not believe John's explanation, or the Book of Hebrews, which speaks of the Heavenly Jerusalem.

But we who are New Testament believing Christians, who believe that the New Testament is part of the inspired Word of God, should have no trouble accepting the fact that God has blessed the Heavenly Jerusalem, rather than the physical city on earth.

The key, of course, is to understand that "*Yerushalayim*" is a plural word, indicating more than one city. Though the Prophets of the Old Testament never mentioned the Heavenly Jerusalem, they prophesied of it nonetheless by use of the plural name. And so when we read the Old Testament, we must seek to know which Jerusalem the Prophets were referencing. As a general rule, when the Prophets spoke of Jerusalem in positive terms, they prophesied of the New Jerusalem. When they spoke of Jerusalem negatively, they spoke of the Old Jerusalem.

The Two Temples

Solomon's temple was the first to be glorified. It prophesied of the greater Temple that was to come. This greater Temple is not a physical temple, but rather the one that Paul described in Ephesians 2:20-22.

> "Having been built upon the foundation of the apostles and prophets, Christ Jesus Himself being the corner stone, 21 in whom the whole building, being fitted together is growing into a holy temple in the Lord; 22 in whom you also are being built together into a dwelling of God in the Spirit." NASB

Paul was speaking of the corporate Temple made up of the entire Body of Christ. Peter says of this Temple, that we are each "living stones"—1 Peter 2:5, used to build it. There is another sense in which we, as individuals, are also a complete Temple in ourselves, for Paul says in 1 Corinthians 3:16.

> "Do you not know that you are a temple of God, and that the Spirit of God dwells in you?" NASB

In this individual sense, we can make the comparison of the three parts of the Temple with the three parts of our being. The Temple consisted of an outer court, the holy place, and the Most Holy Place. Our personal "temples" contain body, soul, and spirit.

The point is to show that in the Old Testament God dwelt in buildings made of wood and stone, but that these were never intended to be the final dwelling place of God. Even Solomon recognized this when he said in 1 Kings 8:27.

> "But will God indeed dwell on the earth? Behold, heaven and the highest heaven cannot contain Thee, how much less this house, which I have built!" NASB

Solomon recognized the impossibility of building an earthly house that could house the glory of God. And so he hinted of a greater Temple that was yet to come, one made of living stones and Holy Spirit callings and ministries ("vessels" and "pillars").

In this new Temple would also be a new order of priests, not of Levi but of Melchizedek. The priests of Levi were a temporary order of priests, called to minister during the time of the Old Covenant. One had to be descended from Aaron to minister in that temple. But in the New Covenant Order, the Melchizedek priests did not have to be descended from Aaron, but from Jesus Christ, not in a natural manner but as spiritual Sons of God.

The Melchizedek priesthood was older than that of Levi. The original king of Salem (Jerusalem) was not of Levi, because he came long before Levi was even born. Years later, David was a priest of the Melchizedek Order, even though he himself was not a Levite—Psalms 110:4.

> "The Lord has sworn and will not change His mind, "Thou art a priest forever according to the order of Melchizedek." NASB

David was of the tribe of Judah, and so he was not eligible to be a Levitical priest, as they had to be of the tribe of Levi. Instead, like the original Melchizedek, he ruled Jerusalem, the "city of Salem." But in the greater sense, all of this prophesied of the New Jerusalem, which would be ruled by David's greater Son, King Jesus.

Jesus Christ was of the tribe of Judah, and so it was not lawful for Him to be High Priest of the order of Levi. He came as High Priest of Melchizedek—Hebrews 7:11-14 says:

> "Now if perfection was through the Levitical priesthood [for on the basis of it the people received the Law], what further need was there for another priest to arise according to the order of Melchizedek, and not be designated according to the order of Aaron? 12 For when the priesthood is changed, of necessity there takes place a change of law also. 13 For the One concerning whom these things are spoken belongs to another tribe, from which no one has officiated at the altar. 14 For it is evident that our Lord was descended from Judah, a tribe with reference to which Moses spoke nothing concerning priests." NASB

Jesus Christ is the High Priest of an entirely new order of priests, whose sacrifice is the Lamb of God alone. Neither the High Priest nor his children, as the sons of God, are eligible by law to offer animal sacrifices, nor are these effective after the Cross.

Jesus is not going to return to the old Jerusalem to be High Priest over Levitical priests making animal sacrifices in a physical temple; no, He is already the High Priest of a New Temple—The Church and High Priest of the New Covenant. The New Covenant is not a temporary interlude after which time the Old Covenant provisions will be reinstated. The Old Covenant was faulty and has become obsolete. The "better" Covenant and its provisions are here to stay. The Bible says that those who promote the old way do not know the mind of Christ—Hebrews 8:13 says:

> "When He said, "A New Covenant," He has made the first obsolete. But whatever is becoming obsolete and growing old is ready to disappear." NASB

The New Covenant, on the other hand, will never grow old, nor will it ever become obsolete. The New Covenant is known as an Everlasting Covenant, and something that is everlasting is just that—everlasting; not having any end!

Judaizing the Church

The Dispensationalist misunderstanding of Scripture has given rise to Christian Zionism, which has re-established the problem Paul faced in the First Century of Judaizing the Church. Prior to the destruction of the temple in the First Century, the early Church continued sacrificing in the temple and submitting to all of the Old Covenant forms which had actually been changed at the Cross. In fact, the Book of Hebrews was written anonymously by the Apostle Paul and directed specifically at them in order to break their dependence upon the Old Covenant, its forms, and its rituals.

Modern Dispensationalism has brought us once again to the same problem Apostle Paul faced in the First Century. The attempt is being made to turn the Church back to the Old Covenant, which would empower Levites to re-institute animal sacrifices in a physical temple in Jerusalem. Like the Jerusalem Church, the Christians are trying to add Jesus to the Old Covenant and its old priestly system.

Such a view may admit that Jesus is the Mediator of the New Covenant in His first coming, but it strongly suggests also that Jesus becomes the Mediator of the Old Covenant in His second coming. There is hardly a doctrine that is more detrimental to the foundations of Christianity than this. It overthrows virtually all what Jesus accomplished on the Cross. It reverses virtually every major change that took place under the New Covenant that is described in the Book of Hebrews.

If this teaching were allowed to stand, the Book of Hebrews would eventually be removed from the New Testament. So we must choose which Jerusalem is to be our "mother." If we choose "Hagar," we will become her sons and fall short of the promises of God. Only by choosing "Sarah," the New Jerusalem, will we be able to be inheritors and co-heirs with Christ.

Father Abraham

Abraham's life provides us with such a tremendous metaphor for our own lives and journey, and as such it would be wise for us to briefly look at this in order to bring greater clarity to our position. As we read Hebrews 11:8-14 there are some similarities to our lives and what the Apostle Paul was conveying in his letters.

> "By faith Abraham obeyed when he was called to go out to the place which he would receive as an inheritance. And he went out, not knowing where he was going. 9 By faith he dwelt in the land of promise as in a foreign country, dwelling in tents with Isaac and Jacob, the heirs with him of the same promise; 10 for he waited for the city which has foundations, whose builder and maker is God. 11 By faith Sarah herself also received strength to conceive seed, and she bore a child when she was past the age, because she judged Him faithful who had promised. 12 Therefore from one man, and him as good as dead, were born as many as the stars of the sky in multitude--innumerable as the sand, which is by the seashore. 13 These all died in faith, not having received the promises, but having seen them afar off were assured of them, embraced them and confessed that they were strangers and pilgrims on the earth. 14 For those who say such things declare plainly that they seek a homeland."

- He knew that he was a stranger or an alien.
- He lived in tents not putting down permanent roots in the earth system.
- He looked for that permanent city whose builder and maker was God—this is an apostolically framed mentality.

Abraham, the father of faith began confessing that they were pilgrims and strangers in the earth. He embraced that which was far off and not earthly (because for all intents and purposes, they were in the Promised Land). He knew that the physical Promised Land was not the real thing but only an allegory and that Heaven was the real deal! He confidently and aggressively pursued the New Jerusalem, known as the Heavenly Jerusalem. We too, like Abraham can aggressively and confidently pursue all that God has for us. We do not need to be bound by an earthly system or be brought under an outdated and extinct Old Covenant, we are under the New Covenant, purchased and ratified by the Blood of Jesus Christ. We do not need the "school master", or Old Testament system any more as we have graduated.

It is my prayer that the Church of Jesus Christ will rise up like Esther of old, like the Apostles and Saints in the Book of Acts and throughout the New Testament, like the Apostles and Saints throughout history and extend the Kingdom of God in every sphere of life. May we be bold and confident as we press towards both the Maturity and Unity of the One Church of Jesus Christ in the earth, in the Mighty and Matchless Name of our Lord and Saviour, Jesus Christ!

OTHER EXCITING TITLES
by Michael Scantlebury

THE FORTRESS CHURCH

According to Webster's English Dictionary "fortress" is defined as: a fortified place: stronghold, *especially*: A large and permanent fortification sometimes including a town. A place that is protected against attack!

This book seeks to describe what is a "Fortress Church". We would be looking into the dynamics of this Church as described in Jacob's vision in Genesis Chapter 28, also as described by the Prophet Isaiah, in Isaiah Chapter 2 and as the one detailed in a Psalm of the sons of Korah in Psalms Chapter 48. We would also be looking at a working model of this type of church as found at Antioch in the Book of Acts. Finally we would be exploring the church at Ephesus, where the Apostle Paul by the Holy Spirit revealed some powerful descriptions of the Church!

For ordering details see the end of this book
Or visit www.wordalive.ca

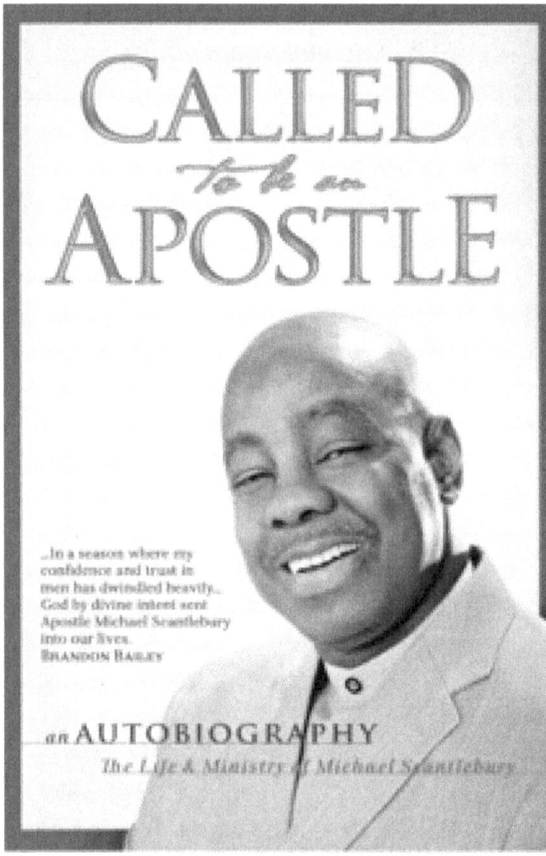

CALLED TO BE AN APOSTLE

This autobiography spans fifty-two years of my life on the earth thus far and I have the hope of living several more… Our home was always packed with young people and we did enjoy times of really wonderful fellowship! Although we were experiencing these wonderful times of fellowship my appetite and desire to grow in the things of God continued unabated. I continued to read anything and everything that I could put my hands on that would strengthen my life. I began reading Wigglesworth, Moody, Finney, Idahosa, Lake, and the list went on and on! But the more I read the more this question burned in my heart—"*why is it that every time we hear/read about a move of God, it is always miles away and in another country? Why can't I experience some of the things that I am reading about?*" Little did I know the Lord would answer that desire!

LEAVEN REVEALED

The Bible has a lot to say about *leaven* and its effects upon the Believer. Leaven as an ingredient gives a false sense of growth. In the New Testament there are at least six types of *leaven* spoken about and we will be exploring them in detail, in order to ensure that our lives are completely free of the first five, and completely influenced by the sixth! These types of leaven include the following: The leaven of the Pharisees; The leaven of the Sadducees; The leaven of the Galatians; The leaven of Herod; The leaven of the Corinthians. However, the Leaven of the Kingdom of God, is the only type of leaven that has the power and capacity to bring about true growth and lasting change to our lives.

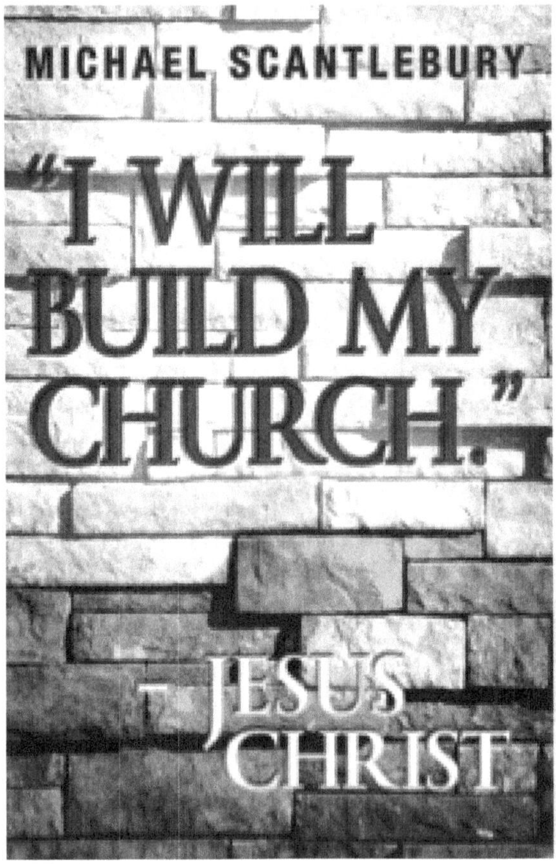

I Will Build My Church. – Jesus Christ

"For we are his *masterpiece*, created in Christ Jesus for good works that God prepared long ago to be our way of life." Ephesians 2:10

What a powerful picture of the Church of Jesus Christ--His Masterpiece! Reference to a *masterpiece* lends to the idea that there are other pieces and among them all, this particular one stands head and shoulders above the rest! This is so true when it comes to the Church that Jesus Christ is building; when you place it alongside everything else that God has created, The Church is by far His Masterpiece

Jesus Christ the Apostle and High Priest

There is a dimension to the apostolic nature of Jesus Christ that I would like to capture in His one-on-one encounters with several people during the time He walked the face of the earth and functioned as Apostle. In this book we will explore several significant encounters that Jesus Christ had with different people where valuable principles and insight can be gleaned. They are designed to change your life!

FIVE PILLARS OF THE APOSTOLIC

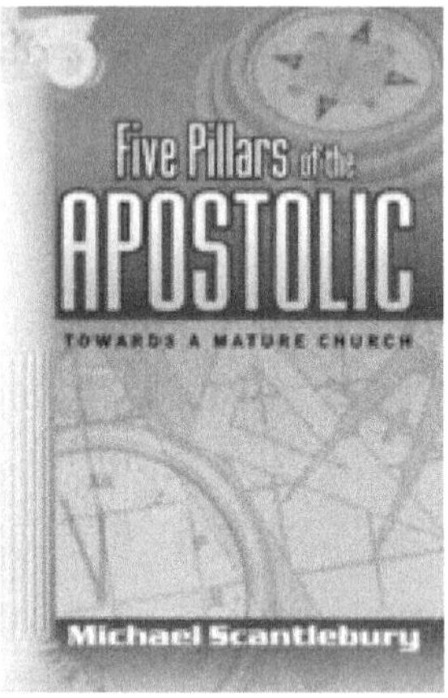

It has become very evident that a new day has dawned in the earth, as the Lord restores the foundational ministry of the Apostle back to His Church. This book will give you a clear and concise understanding of what the Holy Spirit is doing in The Church today!

APOSTOLIC PURITY

In every dispensation, in every move of God's Holy Spirit to bring restoration and reformation to His Church, righteousness, holiness and purity has always been of utmost importance to the Lord. This book will challenge your to walk pure as you seek to fulfill God's Will for your life and ministry!

For ordering details see the end of this book
Or visit www.wordalive.ca

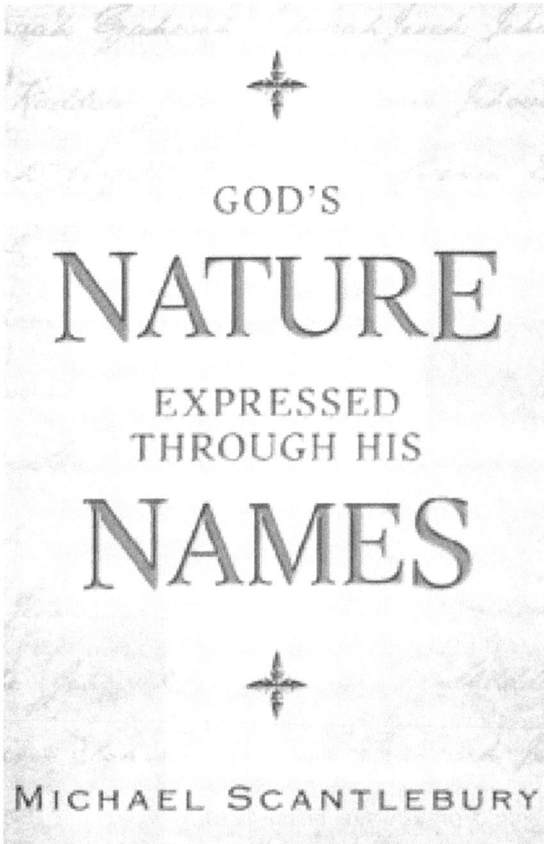

GOD'S NATURE EXPRESSED THROUGH HIS NAMES

How awesome it would be when we encounter God's Nature through the varied expressions of His Names. His Names give us reference and guidance as to how He works towards and in us as His people--and by extension to society! As a matter of fact it adds a whole new meaning to how you draw near to Him; and by this you can now begin to know His Ways because you have come into relationship with His Nature!

INTERNAL REFORMATION

"Internal Reformation" is multifaceted. It is an ecclesiology laying out the blue print of the Church Jesus Christ is building in today's world. At the same time it is a manual laying out the modus operandi of how Believers are called to function as dynamic, militant overcomers who are powerful because they carry internally the very character and DNA of Jesus Christ.

KINGDOM ADVANCING PRAYER VOLUME I

The Church of Jesus Christ is stronger and much more determined and equipped than she has ever been, and strong, aggressive, powerful, Spirit-Filled, Kingdom-centred prayers are being lifted in every nation in the earth. This kind of prayer is released from the heart of Father God into the hearts of His people, as we seek for His Glory to cover the earth as the waters cover the sea.

APOSTOLIC REFORMATION

If the axe is dull, And one does not sharpen the edge, Then he must use more strength; But wisdom brings success." (Ecclesiastes 10:10) For centuries the Church of Jesus Christ has been using quite a bit of strength while working with a dull axe (sword, Word of God, revelation), in trying to get the job done. This has been largely due to the fact that she has been functioning without Apostles, the ones who have been graced and anointed by the Lord, with the ability to sharpen.

Kingdom Advancing Prayer Volume II

Prayer is calling for the Bridegroom's return, and for the Bride to be made ready. Prayers are storming the heavens and binding the "strong men" de-claring and decreeing God's Kingdom rule in every jurisdiction. This is what we call Kingdom Advancing Prayer. What a *Glorious Day* to be *Alive* and to be in the *Will* and *Plan of Father God*! *Hallelujah*!

Kingdom Advancing Prayer Volume III

One of the keys to the amazing rise to greater functionality of the Church is the clear understanding of what we call Kingdom Advancing Prayer. This kind of prayer reaches into the very core of the demonic stronghold and destroys demonic kings and princes and establishes the Kingdom and Purpose of the Lord. This is the kind of prayer that Jesus Christ engaged in, to bring to pass the will of His Father while He was upon planet earth.

IDENTIFYING AND DEFEATING THE JEZEBEL SPIRIT

I declare to you with the greatest of conviction that we are living in the days when Malachi 4:5-6 is being fulfilled. Elijah in his day had to confront and deal with a false spiritual order and government that was established and set up by an evil woman called Jezebel and her spineless husband called Ahab. This spirit is still active in the earth and in the Church; however the Lord is restoring His holy apostles and prophets to identify and destroy this spirit as recorded in Revelation 2:18-23!

SECOND EDITION
VICTORIOUS
ESCHATOLOGY
BY HAROLD R. EBERLE
& MARTIN TRENCH

ORDERING INFORMATION

BOOK ORDERS PLEASE CONTACT:

WORD ALIVE PRESS

Canada | USA:
Phone: 866.967.3782 | Fax: 800.352.9272

International:
Phone: 204.667.1400 | Fax: 204.669.0947
Website – http://wordalivepress.ca

OR FROM:
PRESENT TRUTH MEDIA

Phone: 604.599.3542 | Fax: 604.599.3543
Website – https://present-truthpublishing.com

ALSO AVAILABLE FROM:

www.amazon.com/MichaelScantlebury/e/B008BSTO6Y
www.chapters.Indigo.ca
www.barnesandnoble.com

CPSIA information can be obtained at www.ICGtesting.com
Printed in the USA
LVOW01s0049111213

364731LV00011B/33/P

9 781486 601189